Chilcotin Rose

Mary Kirner of the Wilderness Plateau

Biographical Account of a Wilderness Life

By Arlene Marie Longson

Library and Archives Canada Cataloguing in Publication

ISBN 978-0-9811996-1-0

Printed and Bound by First Choice Books
www.firstchoicebooks.ca

Printed in Canada

Contents

Introduction

Why I came to the Chilcotin plateau could easily be summed up with a quote by Henry David Thoreau. *"I went to the woods because I wished to live deliberately, to front only the essential facts of life, and see if I could not learn what it had to teach, and not when I came to die, discover that I had not lived. I did not wish to live what was not life, living is so dear; nor did I wish to practice resignation unless it was quite necessary. I wanted to live deep and suck out all the marrow of life, to live so sturdily and Spartan-like as to put to rout all that was not life, to cut a broad swath and shave close, to drive life into a corner."* (End Quote)

I was looking for a little place somewhere deep in the woods, where I could be quiet and reflect on my life, relationships, the state of the world, to finish writing a handful of books I'd started, and to be close to wildlife. No matter how hard I tried I couldn't stand the ghastly noise and smells of city life. Even a small city was too loud, too commercial, and far too psychotic. The television had worn me out with all it's shallow fragmented messages and selling, and everywhere I looked I saw people walking around in a state of hypnosis, empty shells, angry at their neighbors, unfulfilled, seemingly lacking something important in their lives. I had to get out of that atmosphere of corporate servitude before I too went mad. My material self had to sit down and negotiate with my creative self to save my own life before the nearest bridge began to look too inviting. What was I willing to settle for to get out of there? As it turned out settling was not what had to do. I was lucky to end up living in a wee log cabin near the Itcha and Ilgachuz Mountain ranges on the Chilcotin Plateau not too far from the Monarch Icefields and Bella Coola on a back-arc volcanic land formation with hundreds of volcanoes and history around me. I exchanged sea level to be four thousand feet above it, where the air is thinner and bread dough takes longer to rise. I'd now live two hundred miles from the nearest traffic light surrounded by Native reserve wild lands; free-range Horse and Cattle country where I could occasionally see men on horseback wearing Bonanza-style kerchiefs over their faces herding Cattle across the highway. A place where not only free range domestic Horses roam but where you might catch a glimpse of the ghost of the wild Spanish Stallion. I went into the heart of Grizzly, Wolverine, Moose, Caribou, you name it, it's here country; a land of famous cowboys and wilderness men and women who wear their hats and boots authentically not as occasional costumes. I would now live next to a lake covered by three feet of ice and have the option of using an ice-road for seven to eight months of the year. I would haul my water in buckets, heat it on a wood stove for cooking, chores, and bathing. I'd split my own firewood, haul and stack a lot of it too although in the beginning I'd have a lot of help with that. My meals would be cooked on a wood stove or open fire in front of my cabin. I'd give up flushing toilets in exchange for a slanted old outhouse and a nightjar. I'd do my laundry by hand in buckets. In summer I'd have the benefit of a garden hose for chores and showering outside and the occasional use of a shower house during the short summer months but would be without both the remainder of the year when everything is frozen solid. And I'd endure temperatures that plummet to minus forty degrees Celcius. This little old log cabin that Mary Kirner's son Robert built when he was a teenager was used for eleven years by a successful wilderness author and she'd left just before my arrival. Later on I'd meet her several times. The cabin sits on the site of a Native war camp right at the location of the famous Chilcotin war where the Smallpox epidemic was given to the Natives with infected blankets. If you scout around a bit you can still find quiggly holes and arrowheads poking out of the soil. Was I running away from something or toward it? For me, it was both and the woman who made it all possible entered my psyche in such a way that I was compelled to put away all the subjects I'd been writing about to tell her story instead. As you flip through the pages of Mary's life you'll find the story of an extraordinary woman and read exclusive eyewitness accounts about the Monarch Ice field tragedy of 1992 and what the media forgot to tell you. You'll brush with bizarre yet real wilderness creatures; find out what Beaver meat tastes like, and how to conduct a Horsefly race. You'll read exclusive details of the feats of four-time World Champion Arm Wrestler Mike Kadar, and go up close with extreme-extreme remote cabin building and planes that go bump. You'll read never before published details of the last days of the legendary John Edwards, son of Ralph Edwards the famous 'Crusoe of Lonesome Lake', and Mary's role helping out the crews during the wildfire that wiped out his family's irreplaceable homestead in 2004. You'll read what she has to say about her friendship with the elusive reclusive John, and much more. This is also a story about charity, tireless devotion to community and family, and about walking the line with nature and wildlife but this is not just a story about a woman who lives in the woods. It is the story of a woman who made an artform out of bringing together two worlds, the city and the wilderness. If you enjoy sordid smut stories, you won't find one here. What you will find is the story of a humble and decent woman living a uniquely special and truly decent life. She's a walking, talking, living treasure, a person so authentic, sturdy, and vivid that her life by its very nature has the power to teach. I had to stop in my tracks and seize what was concrete, larger than life, and verifiable. I had to tell the world and history books about Mary Kirner, the last of an already-rare breed of brawny yet tender women from the living Wild West on the Chilcotin Plateau.

A Rose is Born

Mary's father, August Kirner, was born in Germany and came to the good country when he was just seventeen years old, and he married her mother Lillian who was of English descent, on March 24th 1940. Mary's grandmother had been a baker for the Queen Mother of England's tea parties. Mary was born on February 11th 1941 and she had one sister who was born the following year, on July 1st 1942 in Grand Prairie Alberta. She rode twenty-one miles on horseback to school until she reached grade nine. Her class was small by today's standards with somewhere between twenty-five and thirty students.

Her dad homesteaded, breaking the land by hand, raising Alfalfa, Barley, and mostly every farm-critter you can think of. It was a good life because her family lived mostly off the land, buying only the food they couldn't grow themselves, like coffee, tea, and sugar, which was heavily rationed in the winter months during the war. Toilet paper hadn't been invented yet so trips to the outhouse or bushes required a fistful of catalogue-page-paper and it was a real treat whenever Mandarin and Japanese orange season arrived. The tissue wrap from the oranges made a luxurious change from catalogue pages. She got a good start on her work ethic at a very young age helping with the tough chores, picking weeds and rocks by hand in the fields, always doing her share of the labour. It was hard, sweaty, dirty work, but it had to be done and good lessons learned young stick with you. In Mary's case, those traits are what got her through the tough times later on, when she was on her own with a family to feed. She's exhibited an amazing and admirable strength throughout her life and a person can't help but feel somewhat inferior in the shadow of such a hard worker.

In 1956 her father sold the farm in Grand Prairie, Alberta and moved the family to Abbotsford, British Columbia, where he did what many did back then, he took a job with the railroad. Mary finished high school, went to work, and married in 1961 and began foster-parenting. She bore one natural son she named Clark and proceeded to adopt another son, Robert, and then her only daughter, Connie. Now she had three kidlings and she was set.

In 1969 she decided to leave the rat race. She wanted to buy a wilderness resort at Nimpo Lake, British Columbia, because she loved the tourist and service industry. On top of it all, she loved the Chilcotin country and all that was in it. After the decision had been made to set out and buy a resort she drove the yellow 1967 Dodge crewcab loaded up with her husband and three children the 500-mile trip to Nimpo. They looked at two resorts, Pine Point Resort on the southern tip of the lake, and Nimpo Lake Resort at the north end. Mary and her clan decided to stay at the former while they looked around. The final decision to buy the 80-acre Nimpo Lake Resort was made based on the fact that the other place, Pine Point, was government-leased land. She wanted to buy a place she knew would be hers, where she could stay and raise her family. They bought the resort, then returned to Abbotsford to pack up their worldly possessions.

On June 15th 1969 she said goodbye to her old farming town in the Fraser Valley and piled her husband, daughter Connie, her two sons Clark and Robert, her Dog Rachael, along with three Cats into the old yellow dodge. She turned her sights Northwest, toward the wilderness, a place that she and her family were destined to live and find adventure for at least the next 40 years. The road was paved to Williams Lake, but after that the remaining stretch of desolate highway 20 was rough gravel, which made for a rugged journey up the plateau. The last 30 miles had to be made with a totally flat tire on the rear and the sound of the metal rim grinding into the pot-holed, washboard road. Not long after she arrived she was greeted by her new neighbors, Lenny and Kip Lemke who brought her a gift, a couple of smoked Rainbow Trout, a welcome snack from across the Bay.

New Digs in the Woods

Her new eighty-acre property, which was formerly a ranch with Sheep, Horses, and Cattle, was equipped with an old shack, eight cabins, and a barn. Prior to that, it was the site of a Native war camp. Many Obsidian (volcanic glass) arrowheads and other artifacts are still buried in the soil. Sometimes when the sunrays hit the ground just the right way, a glistening fragment will catch her eye and she adds it to her growing collection. One of the most interesting features of the property are the remains of what once were two old Quiggly holes which were the traditional fire pit or root cellar found in the center of a Native tipi. There was also a long-house still standing on the property, where Tsilhkot'en men once gathered for meetings and other important events. She wondered what stories the land could tell that had never been told!

Mary and her kidlings were now houseless. An old thin-walled summer shack might have been fine for the previous owners because they traveled to warmer climates during the winter months, as so many folks who live around here do. But for Mary, this was to be a challenge that would transform her, and her children's lives. Although it was a tough-go they would look back on those early times many years later with great fondness. There was no warmer climate waiting for this clan. They stuck it out year in and year out, through more than one harsh winter. The first year they lived in the old thin-walled shack and it was mighty cold. Temperatures plummeted to a frigid -60°Celcius. She had the fire roaring, and had to get up many times through the nights to keep it stoked and sometimes she found thick sheets of ice on the walls, inside the shack. The kids woke up one morning to find their goldfish bowl water frozen solid, so keeping the abode warm presented more than a small challenge and really toughened them up. The only salvation was that the air on the plateau is very arid, receiving barely eight to ten inches of precipitation a year, most of it coming down in the form of light powdered snow. Mary made darn sure the kids got fed hearty meals of Moose and Rainbow Trout, fresh, smoked, and canned. Three dozen jars were enough for the entire family over the long freeze-up. Yes, there are colder places on Earth, but not many! Temperatures on the plateau can easily run neck in neck with those at the North Pole, and even the colder South Pole. Winter temperatures at the North Pole can range from about −43 °C (−45 °F) to −26 °C (−15 °F), averaging around −34 °C (−30 °F). The lowest temperature ever recorded on Earth is −89.6 °C, and this was at the South Pole. Once you get to -60°C, it doesn't make much difference anymore, it's dam cold! The Chilcotin Plateau could easily be dubbed the Arctic or Antarctic of British Columbia.

Mary had no electricity or running water so she pumped it from a well into buckets for all her cooking, cleaning, bathing and other chores and then hauled it to the shack by hand everyday. When night fell, candles and oil lamps were lit but doing anything by that kind of light makes you want to sleep, so when those long winter nights rolled around that's what Mary's clan did after dark, they slept. It wasn't as if she had to choose this rugged lifestyle. She wanted it. She possessed a deep need to carve out a wilderness life, so the comforts of Abbotsford weren't missed at all, and as harsh as the first winter was, the worst was in 1975. November 4th, 5th, and 6th were the most trying of days. Every roof had three feet of snow on top and the Anahim Community Hall roof collapsed from the weight of it. Mary drove down on the lake on her snow machine to the cabins on the point and shoveled the snow off, for folks who were away for the winter. No one asked her to do it, she just decided to. In 1993 there was four feet of snow but it hadn't weighed down the roofs like happened in 1975, making that year one for the books in terms of damage.

For a couple of years all three kids rode Horses out to the highway to catch the bus for school. That's a four-kilometer trip up a rough dirt road, most often in snow. When they entered high school they rode the bus to Williams Lake, a four-hour trip. Something kids often did was show up at the bus stop wearing their pajamas. That tradition still hangs today and you'll often see kids riding the four-hour trip (five by bus) to Williams Lake, all sleepy-eyed in their night flannels.

The new house was built in 1971 and Mary was able to move her kids out of the old thin-walled shack. She began pumping water from the well into a tank instead of buckets, which made things easier, but electricity wasn't brought in until 1981. To bring power in, she went out and marked off blocks of trees with colored tape, areas that needed to be logged-off to make way for the power line so she sent Clark out to do it. "He got the colors mixed up and logged off the wrong area. My own son was eighteen years old before I had any clue he was color-blind!" laughed Mary.

When the kids were growing up, it wasn't too often they'd see critters set up housekeeping inside the outhouse, down below, but it wasn't unheard of either. Occasionally Connie would trek off to the potty for a few moments of peace, plop herself down then suddenly jump up, yank her trousers up over her behind like a bolt, and dash outta there, leaving the door flapping behind her. When you're expecting a little privacy it can be quite a shock to hear goings-on down in the muck. Darn skunks were raising their families right down in there. Of all the places a creature could set up a den, why on Earth would a mama skunk select a place with such a stench? Maybe a skunk rationalizes that if she makes her home right in the poop she might never have to use up her own musk fending off predators, thereby keeping her young-uns safe from harm. Makes perfect sense if you think about it, but you may not want to sit down on the potty too suddenly for fear you might scare that mama into letting go her vast reserves. She'd have a good line of sight for aim and you could end up walking around smelling a bit rich for a while. When it was known there was a skunk down below, trips to the john were quick, calculated, and as non-intrusive as possible.

It takes a certain kind of woman to live and stick it out in the wilderness and a certain kind of man to remain strong and true to his woman beyond his second childhood, a problem that plagues wilderness husbands as much as city men. They work dam hard and it can take a toll, so the men often find relief hunting, fishing, building log cabins, flying airplanes, and huddling together over a deck of cards and a few jokes, spewing off fumes amidst the booze, tobacco, and tall tales. But the vast quiet of an endless natural landscape can turn a man's head around, making true the tales that the Chilcotin is hard on women and Horses. Men often put-down or leave their Horses, and they leave their women too, looking toward the concrete jungle for whatever they thought they'd missed living in the woods whiling away their years with the Bears, Moose, isolation and toil. They often sit in the bush dreaming of excess, city women, warmer climates, and finer wines. Not that the wine doesn't flow like a river in the woods because it sure enough did, and the evidence of that can be seen along the hundreds of miles of highway through the Chilcotin in the form of roadside wooden-crosses and fresh flower markers. A man often wants what he thinks he doesn't have. Even if what he wants is right under his nose, he thinks it has to be somewhere else. This male phenomenon was destined to strike Mary's life more than once. Burying herself in work was generally touted as a means to forget the ills of life and this couldn't be more true anywhere else than in the wild. There's much work to do, rain, ice, snow, wind, or shine. No matter what else is going on or not going on, animals still have to be fed and their pens cleaned, firewood to split, meals to cook, and family to tend to. If you've been left with three young-uns to raise by yourself, the essential workload is a might bit harder. Many women would just abandon the woods and haul the kids back to the city for an easier life, but not Mary. There was no question but that she was determined to raise her children real, healthy, strong, and good and she proceeded to do just that, probably doing a better job of it on her own than if the male-sort had stayed on. There would be plenty of time later to decide if she would want a new man around or not. In the meantime, she would spend some obligatory time in private grief, and seem a bit quiet or distant from time to time. But through it all she would increase her time spent with friends, being kind to strangers, and tending her hobby farm. She'd cook more for passing-bellies and embrace the romance that exists in nature. This turned out to be, for her, even more rewarding, more soothing, and without a doubt more peaceful and beautiful.

If there ever existed in the world a pure example of unadulterated romance, it could be found in the heart of Mary and her relationship to the land. She awakes each day and fills her environment with her own brightness. You'd never see a hint of anything wrong. She gave herself to nature and the community, which in-turn gave back a bounty of gifts. She'd make a meal for some group and the next thing you know those folks are at her door with armfuls of freshly harvested veggies from their gardens. This exchange was symbiotic and perpetual, and extremely contagious, literally viral, with no stops! You get what you give! Once a week for a couple of years she tried her hand at a mobile bakery business and parked her truck at one of the local grocery stores offering her delicious homemade jelly-filled, sprinkled-sweet donuts, chocolate covered bear-claws, buns, bread, and cookies filled with chunks of chocolate and nuts. Her daughter Connie remembers it well as most do, the delectable treats she made. The first day she was open for business it was on her fortieth birthday. She soon added to her list of titles when she became the local Avon lady, delivering catalogues and taking cosmetic orders from Anahim and Nimpo, all the way to Tatla Lake. Of all the stories told and books written about the people, lifestyles, and history of this Chilcotin Plateau, this woman would prove her abilities time and again, standing the test of 40 years, lending comfort, food, and kindness to friends, resort guests and passers-through. You could talk to most anyone who has lived in this remote and timeless wilderness and they would say she has been an important agent for change in countless lives, young and old, rich and poor. She has been the glue of the social fabric in her tiny community and many of its surrounding areas for as long as most people can remember, She's been a bridge between diehard wilderness cowboys and city slickers, bringing them all together. Her house is one of the few places you'll find the unbathed and the freshly shaved, both vagrant and well-to-do sitting on a couch engaged in conversation. One day she'll have the poorest woods folks sitting at the dinner table sharing a meal and a glass of wine with a few wealthy manicured city folks and the next day she'll be out raising funds for sick children or cooking a meal for a hundred people. She's always doin' for somebody. It isn't unusual to find her at the Anahim cemetery weeding the graves of passed-away guests who visited her resort over the years and had chosen to be buried nearby. It's not a big cemetery by anyone's standard. You can count the folks who rest there on one hand. She's mastered the art of neutrality, kindness, and second chances in her own life and in doing so created a climate of peace between opposites and adversaries. Often without saying a word, her smile, body language, daily actions, and life radiate outward spawning a contagious energy that spreads to everyone she meets. She teaches, leads, and communicates by example and people pay attention. When you witness folks spending a lot of time with her, you can see changes in them. It's as though they adopt her animations and expressions, even in the way they deliver a conversation, do a good deed, or hand you a cup of coffee. There's a little bit of her shining in everyone. It's as if the Chilcotin is a population of people who are, or at least try to be reflections of Mary. It's a tough job though, trying to do the things she does year in and year out. It would be a lot of work maintaining a spirit as full of life as hers if it didn't come to you naturally. You'd be hard pressed to meet a single person that could be as consistently good. She's a stand-alone at not much more than 5' 5 ½ inches tall, 140 pounds, with deep-blue eyes and short light brown hair with a touch of snow on the roof. She's casually dressed and her appearance can be deceiving. She looks, walks, and talks just like a woman, but her muscle and determination can match and surpass that of most men. Her reasoning and intellect are surprisingly sharp and well developed for a country girl who hasn't seen much of the fast lane. In the wink of an eye she can solve most problems without much thought, and when called upon for advice of most any nature she'll roll a solution off her tongue as fast as you can ask the question. Most times the answer she gives is a good one that would take most people many hours, days, or even weeks of contemplation to figure out. It is said, that these woods are hard on Horses and women but she shatters that folklore looking no-worse-for wear than a woman of 40 years. Her vibrant tireless energy leaves most in her dust. Today at sixty-nine, she's every bit the busy Matriarch of the community she was in her younger days. With a quiet unassuming hand she continues to influence friends, family, strangers, underprivileged children, wild and domestic animals, the landscape, history, and flowers! Her home wouldn't be complete without foliage and she collects blooms of all descriptions. To walk into her wilderness home which displays a painted sign on its outer front that reads, 'Mary's Place', smack-dab in the middle of thirty or forty below zero weather, you enter an oasis world of full-color-bloom. The dead of winter is no trouble for her Cactus Orchids, and Geraniums sprawling around her massive windows that offer a close-up panoramic spectacle of the lake. It makes me wonder if maybe she sings to them when no one is lookin', or maybe its just her vibrant, assuring, and safe energy that makes them want to offer themselves up for her pleasure.

Fall on the Plateau

Summer comes and goes short and sweet, and is famously intensely bug-ridden. The seasonal shift is marked by sudden change. One day the bugs are swarming and there are lush greens everywhere, and the next day there's frost on the ground, a diminishment of flying insects and a different feel about the place, different smells and everything that was green is yellow, orange, brown, and red. Come the end of September into early October the air really has a biting-chill. The loosened leaves break free from the Poplars and scatter in the breeze, which is punctuated by an airy sea of exploding white willow-seed-packets releasing their fluff and they set to drift like hapless furry quarters floating this way and that way. Each has the same purpose but a different destination and could be said to represent a wish, or a dream for new life, carrying the embryos of tomorrow embedded in the memory of a rainbow-summer just gone by. Some willow packets are destined for half-full buckets of rain and the water's skin catches them as they pass by. They gather and clump and are pushed around on the surface in a delicate ballet. And they collect in your hair like dry snow, and in your memory as dream-fodder for later, something to reflect on through the long bitter winter which begins to set-in noticeably by the beginning of October, or sometimes earlier in mid September. Breathing is risky, you have to be careful you don't inhale the fluffs, for even one flake caught in your windpipe can curse you into a fit of coughing that lingers all day. And while you're coughing, you better not inhale another one or you'll be coughing for a week.

Once fall quiets the land the non-resident transient wildlife become restless settling in groups on treetops and down in the willows preparing to move on to warmer places as other more hearty beasts arrive and begin setting up their winter dens. There's no mistaking the changing of seasons here, especially winter which comes on the blade of a knife. Geese, Blue Birds, Finches, Fly Catchers, Kinglets, Warblers, most of the song birds, including the Swallows, Grackles, Red-Winged and other types of Blackbirds, Sandpipers, and Sandhill Cranes have begun to migrate. Some Mallard and other Ducks, Loons, Owls, Eagles, Hawks, Chickadees, Whiskey Jacks (Camp Robbers/Gray Jays), and Woodpeckers still seem to hang-about looking for any scrap of food they can find. In the end only a few daring souls stay behind and many of them won't survive.

A knarly, twisted Beaver lodge sits in the middle of the swampy meadow next to Mary's Place and the Trumpeter Swans begin announcing their arrival with their trademark honks. Over-sized Ravens and even a few Crows begin to pass through, usually with a glance down at the meadows to see if there might be a tidbit to eat, but usually they pass without stopping. By early November the Loons are gone and many raptor species begin to take their hunting more seriously than they did in the summer months. Rodents are burrowing and are harder to catch and a hooked-beak has to put more energy into catchin' anything. Pygmy, Great Horned, and the occasional Snowy and Gray Owl scour by day and night in search of Chickadees. The occasional Blue Heron and one or two Mountain Stellars, a Grackle, a Red-Winged Blackbird, a couple of Grouse, and a pair of Bald Eagles still hang about even though they've already devoured all of the baby Loons Mary adored. The odd Duck and Goose still zing overhead, but a neighbor from across the lake has decided to bring a lame-winged Canada Goose over to Mary and she put him in with the Chickens, Peacocks, and Guinea Hen to see how he'll do. After a bit of R&R and Mary's TLC the Goose left the coop and flew off.

The high altitude of Mary's home lends itself to arid seasons. She receives only about ten inches of rain each year. The air and volcanic-land is dry and the soil thin, so the vast expanse of trees claim their nutrients not so much from the soil, as from the forest canopy itself. This creates an extremely unique ecosystem, one that shows the results of the Mountain Pine Beetle that have devoured much of the Pines of British Columbia by now, encompassing an area the size of Sweden. But many more Spruce and Poplar shoot up out of the ground and quickly fill in the gaps. The Chilcotin was hit hard during the years 2005-2006, so Mary and Logan set about taking down some of the dead ones for firewood. You can't leave them standing, just weaving in the wind because after only a year or two they become loose in the root and a threat to the human skull. It's best not let danger gather. Logan eyeballs the tree and decides where he wants to put it, then sets to work. He can put a tree down right between two parked cars without scratching the paint. Mary religiously gathers up the branches and pinecone debris and tosses it into her bonfire. Day in and day out the sound of chainsaws going, and the crack of trees hitting the ground are the highlights of the day.

Eight thousand remote lakes dot the Chilcotin and countless pristine rivers, creeks, and streams carve their way through, many of them still unnamed. The watercolors of the sky, lakes, and decaying leaves transform into whipped cream and sugary frosted snow that stays from early November through to the end of May. Without fail there is ice on the lake by Halloween. As the first week of November rolls around and temperatures really began to drop, the sound of frigid lake-water lapping up against newly forming ice can clearly be heard near the mouth of Nimpo creek where it dumps into the lake. From a bit of a distance the sound of the water breaking on the growing ice shelf as it creeps out from the shore sounds like birds chattering, bamboo wind-chimes, or tin cans tied to the back of a wedding car. Run-off from an early snowfall followed by a temporary unexpected melt has swollen the creek. Sounds like a commotion. The lake begins to accumulate several feet of ice and is quickly covered over with snow-dump after snow-dump, which has to be plowed regularly to keep the ice-road open. Now is the time for local bush pilots to think about taking the floats off their planes and attaching their skis.

Every marvelous breed of predator and prey can be seen from Mary's window cutting across the ice, Moose, Caribou, Deer, Otter, Muskrat, Beaver, Coyote, Wolf, Wolverine, Mink, Weasel, Rabbit, Squirrel, Ptarmigan, and Fishers. The Cougar and Bobcat are elusive but nonetheless present, always stealthing the perimeter while the Grizzlies and Black Bear sleep-off their fat. The appearance of discreet, well-maintained little clusters of Muskrat hutches begin to protrude from the lake-ice. Ravens, Owls, Eagles, Falcons, and Hawks move through the trees looking to fill their cold sunken bellies.

On her way to town Mary stops her truck to let a Lynx cross her path. On her way home she stops and examines his tracks in the snow so she'll be able to identify him if he ever makes an appearance at her Chicken barn. She hopes he never does, because that would be the end of him.

Winter Wood & Fire

Around mid October Mary's duties really shift gears. You can see the coordination between her activities and the changes in the land itself, and she thoroughly enjoys the synchronicity She removes her Resort signage down off its hinges at the turnoff to her four-kilometer dirt-road for the winter months and then Beetle-kill tree cuttin' goes into full swing. A few green Poplars are snagged for the fish smoker but she takes mostly Pine for her firewood needs. The Beavers, are a big help sometimes, they can log-off a small tree-stand while you're sleepin'. If you float down the lake in a canoe, it's easy to see the effect a single Beaver can have on a Poplar grove. In some spots, the shoreline is nothin' but a mess of fallen chewed-up trees. It's a good thing Poplar sprouts up as fast as it does, which might be nature's way of compensating.

Mary loves nothing more than to hike off by her lonesome early in the morning and clean up the leftover debris from the previous days' cutting and burning. Aside from the relaxation she enjoys tossing branches and Pinecones into a big pile of flames leaping up into the sky, she points out that she dabbles in fire for good reason. She may be a firebug (some would say she's a controlled arsonist), but she's also a fire expert stemming from years of experience, which explains how she manages to confidently interact with it on a regular basis without so much as a spark getting away on her. She knows that a bit of well-placed burning is very good for the soil and that a Pinecone seed won't become fertile without exposure to fire. She says, "Have you seen how many Pinecones there are on a single tree? If even half of them were to germinate, the land would be choked with Pine trees!" With one eye constantly on the weather and simultaneously eyeballing the moisture content of the ground (which can change within hours), she also keeps tabs on the wind speed and direction. Fire has become second nature to her. She goes about her October spot-scorching like a kid at play, and you can hear the orange flames crackling, and pinecones popping from a distance. To catch a glimpse of her torching-up the sky and hear the sound of dry-needle-fuel hitting the flames makes you wanna get out there and do some. She just makes it look so fun. Ahh but many of us lazy-sorts are content to watch. Mary's firework has maintained the land here for nearly 40 years. You'll often find her by herself raking up cones and branches, just puttering around a big bonfire with her blue eyes contrasting her wind-brushed heat-rosy cheeks. It beats wearing face makeup, which is something she does not do. Just because she sells the stuff doesn't mean she has any want or need for it. But she just loves fire, so anytime there's something to burn you can see that flame-thrower's gleam in her eye. September always brings the itch to go out and burn stuff and she gets antsy waiting for the last guests to leave so she can shut down the resort. "I can't wait for this to be over so I can start messin' with trees!" she said excitedly.

One day, I heard what sounded like a large tree, crack and fall hard against the ground. I went outside my cabin to see what was going on. Of course I knew right away when I saw Mary at the lake's edge. It was Logan dropping another Pine Beetle killed tree. As I poked my head out the cabin door into the sub zero morning air I could hear it, that unmistakable brisk buzzing and whine that immediately follows Mary firing-up her chainsaw and going straight to work. I donned an extra layer of socks, pants, a wooly cap, some gloves and moved quickly to get in line behind Connie who was following Mary down the trunk pullin' loose branches out of the way as she bucked off the twisted Old Man's Beard Moss smothered limbs. Logan was bucking up the top end and Connie was running to grab the cone-heavy branches. She'd haul them over to a pile and whoever got there first with a match lit the fire. I'd get in line and start hauling branches and piling them up on the fire, of course I accidentally and unwillingly sacrificed a good glove or two to the fire gods. The flames would rapidly escalate to a certain point, then the wind would suddenly change direction and heads would turn to assess the risk. It wasn't uncommon to smell burning hair. We'd all look around to see who was on fire. Me, being a beginner and all, you had to keep your eyes peeled to make sure I didn't explode. Mary just walked right through the blazing tongues, occasionally waving a bit of smoke away from her face but overall paid little if any worry about her own flammability. When you've been building fires for 40 years, you get to know what's a threat and what isn't. Without lookin' she'd just brush one hand over her arm, shoulder, and head now and then to dampen any stray sparks in case they were there, then she'd reposition her chainsaw and get back to cutting.

If there is one thing Mary despises it's stopping a job before it's finished. I don't want to whine about fatigue or look like a wimp, I want to keep up, and how could any of us forty-something's possibly justify stopping for rest while Mary continues on with the energy and strength of a twenty year-old? It's a tad embarrassing!

One Saturday morning I strolled past her while she was starting a fire and Logan was bucking up a dead tree he had just downed. An hour later Connie arrived at the diminishing flame with a stunned look on her face. Much to her dismay the work was already done and the fire was smoldering. I too had arrived at the tail end of the job and was lucky to find a few toothpicks left on the ground to toss in the flames. Connie, sporting her pout said, "I thought you weren't going to start right away. You said an hour but you're already done? Is there any more to do?" It was like watching one pyromaniac complaining to the other that she had been left out of the crime. Mary just shrugged her shoulders because she knew Connie and I had been visiting earlier and she didn't want to wait. She was happy to just get the job done. She takes a lot of pride in being able to get up bright eyed and bushy-tailed first thing in the morning and get her blood flowing. She doesn't do it to prove anything to anyone. She loves work for its own sake.

One February morning there was a foot of snow on the ground and Mary fell a large tree and bucked into pieces and lit a fire. She was on the move cleaning up and burning debris as surefooted in the snow as any Cat fording a hill, wielding a surprising measure of control and skill, the kind you'd expect from a man who had been in the logging business all his life. "Anything I can do without asking a man to do, I do myself," she said busting into a fresh humble side-grin. That day most of her firewood gathering was for me. I didn't have it hauled to my cabin by the next morning (lazy snail), so here comes Mary in her snow machine towing a sled, hauling a load to my door. I had to really get a move on to be of any use. Be ready by 9:00 AM precisely or she'll just do it herself. If you show up to help, fine, if you don't, you don't. It gets done.

Day after day, I'd drive my truck up to her place to get water and I'd see her out there with a splitting maul in her hand bustin' firewood to stove-sized logs. "Where's Logan?" I asked thinking he could maybe do some for her. She raised the maul up in the air and as she brought the sharp blade down on the block she said, "Oh, he's out on his snow machine for the day!" I stood in amazement watching her split all that firewood like she was shaving shards of butter off a block. "That's one thing I've always done and always will do, is get my own firewood," she said as she brought the maul down and split another log. You can't get her to take a break while she's in the middle of workin'. You just have to wallow in your guilt that she's doing it and you're standing there not doin' it. But if she's been at it for six days in a row and you tell her to take a break or suggest she do the rest the next day, you might convince her. "If I can't get a job done in six days the seventh isn't gonna make much difference so I might as well take some time and do something else. Tomorrow I'm on strike," she says. You might take that to mean she was going to actually sit down and rest, but her version of rest and yours, I guarantee, are not the same. Hers might include things like cooking for 20 people, helping out with some fundraiser, or just being with family for a time. Sometimes she'll just take her grandson Niko by the hand and wander off into the bush to explore, giving him a head start on how to appreciate nature, the animals, and the land.

After a vigorous week she treats herself to a special sinful breakfast and whips up some waffles with peanut butter, strawberries, or peaches slathered in whipped cream and syrup. She loves to indulge in a little bit of Mexican and Chinese once in a while too. She'll eat Chicken but won't touch a boiled egg. Here she is a Chicken farmer gathering eggs every day but she won't eat one. She'll eat scrambled eggs or enchiladas from time to time but she's not a big egg-eater. People drive from miles around to pick up a dozen or two, and they love 'em because of the beautiful deep orange yolks, a sure sign of a healthy egg.

She likes to sip a spirit or two after a long day of working outside. She'll take her favorite drink, famous Grouse Brand Scotch, or a little Bailey's in her coffee, sometimes even in the morning if the day is right. Or maybe a little Brandy if there's someone to share it with, which there usually is by 4:00 in the afternoon when her famous Happy Hour kicks in. Folks usually show up from all around the lake for an hour of conversation and some light sipping, but then it's done and supper is on the go. Happy Hour never turns into a drunken bash. "A glass of wine always tastes better at your place than mine for some reason." I told her. "Well, that's because you shared it with somebody!" she replied. Come to think of it, she's right, and here I thought it might have been the high altitude that made it taste so good. One sentence out of her mouth is worth a dozen hours of useless jabber from a lot of folks and probably many hours of my own useless problem solving. It seems all anyone really needs to do to solve the toughest knots in life is to take a 15 minute consult with Mary and a glass of wine, and you're cured.

But then there's another kind of drink you could have with Mary, if you're a kid that is. As good-luck would have it she was blessed with a few grandchildren. Now Connie brought her little three-year old boy from the city to be exposed to a wholesome back-to-basics upbringing, so he could be around Mary and learn about her 'certain' way of life, and to be in touch with the land like she was when she was growing up. After having been away for twenty years or so she was glad to be back home but there were a few hard and necessary lessons Niko would have to learn, and fast. Living around a lake has its dangers and the only way to keep a kid from sneaking off into the water-zone of no return when no one is lookin', is to teach him what ice water is and what it feels like to suddenly be in it. Little boys don't often listen when they're told to get off the dock or to stop leaning over the side and they have a tendency to get into trouble. So the lesson came not too long after the decision was made to teach it. Little Niko fell into the frigid water and Mary was right there and hauled him up onto the shore. Once he met up with a good bone-chilling polar dip, he didn't want to do that again. It was a tactic that worked for a while, but in mid April when there was still ice on the lake and the melting winter land still had a foot or two of snow left in some places, Mary took him down to the water's edge to rake up a few twigs, decaying Pine needles and cones. For some reason that boy decided he could walk on water and stepped out on the thinning ice and plunged in. She bent down and casually fished him out and took him inside and peeled off his wet duds. She picked off the layer of black Mosquito larvae that was stuck all over him and dumped him into a warm tub. She had a good chuckle over his bold, adventurous spirit but figured he'd probably learned his lesson this time.

Bloody Nosed Assassin

November 29th 2006, Mary went down to the barn to do her usual chores. Everything seemed quite ordinary as she prepared to feed and water the Chickens and give treats to her Llamas. When she arrived at the pen she was surprised to see a Great Horned Owl inside the cage sitting on a Chicken perch. It was a good thing the birds were inside the barn for the winter and not out there or he'd have gotten what he came for. She could have handled him on her own but it is always better to have two people on a job like that, so she fetched Logan to come down and help her deal with the would-be assassin.

When they arrived back at the barn, the Owl was still in the pen and seemed confused as to how to find his way out. Logan put on his thick leather gloves and moved toward the beautiful feathered creature of the night and herded him in one direction and then another, trying to persuade him toward the exit. But the Owl became increasingly confused, flying from one end of the cage to the other, banging his nose hard as he slammed up against the wire. Then, he'd grab the wire with his talons and hang upside down, just swinging back and forth up there. When he rotated his head around 180 degrees he revealed a dripping bloody nose. He looked like someone hit him with a boxing glove. After a bit of running around trying to position him to where he'd be able to see a clear path out the gate, the Owl finally dropped down onto the snow-covered ground. Logan crouched down and calmly angled-up beside him and grabbed his feet, one hand on each leg to get those wicked looking claws of his under control. "I've found that you don't have to be too concerned about the beak. The beak is a cutting tool but the talons are the real weapon!" he said as he calmly gripped the Owl by his ankles and held him on top of the gate. After the Owl settled down, he carried him over to the fence and propped his feet along the top. The Owl spread his wings and Logan released his feet and he took off toward the tree line where he vanished behind the workshop.

Over the years there have been occasional Owl troubles at Mary's Place. Back when Robert was a boy it was his job to shut the Chickens in the barn at night so the Coyotes couldn't get them. They like to stalk a Chicken-yard around daybreak. One time Robert shut the door and Mary went off to feed the Cows. Suddenly she realized something wasn't quite right. It was too quiet over at the Chicken house so she made her way back to the coop and peered inside, and there she saw a fright, a Great Horned Owl sitting on a Chicken perch and there wasn't a moving Chicken in sight. The door must not have been closed tight enough and once is all it takes! Her eyes wandered around the barn analyzing the crime scene and she saw two piles of Chickens, one in each corner of the coop. And another bunch of terrified, shivering Chickens piled on top of more terrified, shivering Chickens. The Owl had slaughtered seven and had eaten the breast meat out of six. Talk about a blood bath. She ran off to fetch Logan and that was the end of that Owl. "It was one for one that time! You can always tell it's an Owl by the big pile of fluff left behind. If it's a Coyote who did the deed, he just snatches the Chicken and runs off. A Coyote in a field can find a Mouse under 23 inches of snow," she explained.

Flutter in the Hand

With the season's first Willow leaves the Hummingbirds begin showing up at Mary's feeders. I was at her house picking up my ration of eggs (as others who inhabited my cabin before me did) as these tiny souls zinged back and forth past the kitchen window, staying at the feeder only for a few brief seconds before disappearing to wherever Hummingbirds flit to. Not more than two minutes after I went out the door, I started filling buckets of water from an outdoor tap below the window and was preparing to load them into the back of my truck and haul them to my cabin. She popped open the window above me, leaned out with her arms extended and her hands carefully cupped together and said, "You want to see a Hummingbird?" She slowly opened her hands and revealed the long thin needlelike beak of a wee Hummingbird that had managed to sneak through the door as I was making my exit. Must have been faster than a blink because I never even saw him go past me. She held him as if he were a fragile leaf of rice paper then released him into the wind. Seeing him fly-off, was poetry.

It must have been the end of April or early May when her box of chicks arrived in the mail. Tiny light yellow little balls of fluff, her next generation brood of egg-layers. She set them up in a heated cardboard box in the living room and her cats never touched a-one-of-them; needless to say, aside from the wild birds and rodents they eat, those same cats do enjoy a baby rabbit kill from time to time, but never touched a baby chick. Mary spent the next couple of weeks maintaining their box and cleaning their bums before they were big enough to mix with the other Chickens. Connie stepped in while Mary was away for a day or two, and cleaned their bums. When I say clean their bums, I mean to say that the poop builds up until it's glued on like cement probably from the heat of the lamp inside their incubator-box. It takes a lot of hot water, paper towels, and patience to soak it loose.

Come late May and into early June when the ice clears off the lake, it seems every sort of bird a person can imagine begins showing up around Mary's Place and could be thought of as a virtual bird sanctuary. Everything from Hummingbirds and Red-Winged Blackbirds to the true Bluebirds-Of-Happiness can be seen flitting around in the trees and willows. She said it was Mary Lemke who taught her how to identify birds and she's been observing and feeding them ever since, doing her part to give nature a hand when food supplies are scarce. In one small area you could find all the above birds as well as at least three kinds of Woodpeckers, Chickadees, Canaries, Osprey, Bald Eagles, Geese, Ducks, Loons, Camp Robbers, Swallows, and you can hear the odd Grouse beating his wings in the brush, still trying to lure a mate. It seemed, this year at least, this Grouse love-call would go unanswered. He'd spend the rest of the season alone while all the other birds nested and sported their young freely around him. He might have had a mate, but with the high number of predators around one could expect a Grouse or two to go missing. These little avian critters would even alight occasionally on a nearby lawn-chair to ask for a morsel of Mary's scrambled Chicken's egg or a bit of cheese. This can become a habit, giving handouts to the wild birds at Mary's Place. You become so inundated with birds at such close-range all you really want to do is feed them.

Mary's domestics roam the land freely and her mateless Guinea Hen hangs out with the Peacocks, spending his time yackin'. The Chickens kick-up dust clouds looking for snacks and if they see you coming at a distance they gather together and come running, clucking, cooing and cawing quietly in a very friendly tone. When not socializing they dig little holes in the dirt, nestling in around the cabins, covering themselves with dust to stay cool. The baking-heat of the day can really slow a body down. The Peacocks leap up onto the window ledges of cabins full of guests and sit there lookin' through the window at the people inside, usually yellin' at 'em, but they seem to enjoy the rare spectacle. It's a common thing, to look out your cabin window and see the eyeballs of a Llama or Peacock peering in at you! Just Mary's little angels is all they are!

Although the Robins are larger and more formidably sized here in the Chilcotin, they just hop about the ground pulling up worms and bathing in puddles, flapping their wings in the soupy mud as if it were a fresh waterfall. Not picky I guess, or maybe it keeps the bird-sized Mosquitoes off. The Robins pretty much mind their own business though, only picking on each other now and then.

By early to mid-June Mary's Place is alive with Bees and Horseflies buzzing, Mosquitoes dive-bombing in swarms, Monarchs as well as a plethora of other Butterflies flutter about seemingly aimlessly like bits of toilet tissue. But those Yellow Jackets, Bald Faced Wasps, and Mosquitoes can really drive you to violence. Mary doesn't mind them much though, probably because she's lived with them for nearly 40 years. If she didn't learn to accept them she wouldn't have been able to stick it in the Chilcotin because voluminous biting bug swarms are just a normal unavoidable part of life here. She refuses repellent of all kinds even when folks all around her slather themselves with it every few minutes. She'll swat every now and then when she's talking to you, but forgets it right after.

By mid-June the itty-bitty Blackflies come on thick, bitin' for your flesh. Now those Mary doesn't like much at all! Ahhh, but nothing takes your mind off those vectors knawing and sucking on your flesh like the sight of a fresh spray of tiny Jacob's Ladder blossoms crawling up a knoll. Or the hearty Indian Paintbrush, delicate Wild Roses, Fireweed spears sprouting everywhere! Even the common Dandelion is a sight to behold because of their vast blanket spread. When they flower, you'll find large docile Honeybees lazily settling on almost every golden crown, and when they go to seed, there's a panorama of fluff tumbling over the grasses. Even the slightest breeze sends them aloft. They collide, twin together, and continue sailing along. All this is occasionally interrupted by the unmistakable sound of the infinite-logger, the Beaver at work. You hear the slap of a tail hitting hard on the water nearby. He not so sneakily puts up his fort, damming up the Creek, which some human, usually Mary will hafta tear down, only to return the next morning and find it built all the way up again.

Diane and Lars who stay in one of her waterfront cabins every year for about a five-week stretch, just happened to have come out of their cabin and were walking along the gravel road as I pulled my truck alongside them during the latter part of May 2006. Blood suckers flocked around their heads and they swatted their own faces as we introduced ourselves. After each of us squashed a number of 'squitoes, we got to talking. "They're out in force already!" I said, thinking that a fitting name for the Chilcotin in summer could easily be 'Bug-Tussle', a name my father had given to a little cabin he lived in at 100-Mile House back in the 80's. Lars casually brushed one of those sucking vermin off his cheek and Diane shook her head and smiled, "No, not yet," she replied. "So they get worse?" I asked. She nodded and laughed, "Yeah, later on they do!" Not much later, I might add, because it seems to me it was only a day or two later that very thing happened. Snooping around for info for my book, I asked Diane what she thought about Mary. "One thing that stands out about Mary is that the moment you first arrive here she makes you feel like you just belong here! Not many people or places in the world give you that feeling. Mary's a national treasure! She does so much all the time. See how she keeps the rivers open so the fish can come in? She's a conservation officer all by herself!" she smiled seriously.

And The Wind Bloweth

Comes a blustery day in April, 12:30 in the afternoon and I hear a voice caught up in the whirling gusts circling my cabin. "Hey-llo!" I stuck my head out the sagging screen door and saw her standing there on the long mud-flattened hay-like yellow grass with her short hair trying to blow this way and that way. It was Mary and she'd walked over to get the ladder I borrowed several days earlier but lazily forgot to return. My smokestack cover had blown off in the night over my chimney for the second time and I had to climb up and put it back on, a trick Mary had shown me back in January when I first arrived but I was too scared to do it. I was just about to brag to her that I had managed to get up there and do it myself for a change instead of calling her to do it, but she had that darn ladder on her mind. "You forgot to bring back mah ladder!" she said with just the right measure of playful but firm admonishment in her voice as she came out from the other side of my cabin with the ladder in question resting on her shoulder. "I was going to bring it back to you when I come to get water today!" I replied guiltily. "I'm gonna wash me windows!" she exclaimed. Here you have an extremely blustery day, with 20 km per hour winds with surprise gusts at least double that speed thrusting unpredictably from one direction or the other, and all she can think about is climbing 15-20 feet up a ladder to wash half a dozen 6x7 foot windows. I don't need to spell out the obvious danger in that idea, but whenever I hear she's going to do something precarious I have to stop and think, what is clearly dangerous for other folks is just normal for her. I mean to say the wind blew so forcefully that the brand new dock she and Logan had put out on the lake over the Easter weekend crashed and banged against the ice so hard it wreaked havoc on the wood. Logan ran over and grabbed a neighbor to help get the thing sitting properly again or it would have been destroyed. And then there's Mary up a darn ladder washing windows! Maybe she was doin' it for her plants and flowers so they'd get enough light to keep them blooming. Needless to say, I tried to deliver my humble apologies for keeping her ladder too long but she was already hoofing it back to her place by the time the words fell out of my mouth. All I saw was her back and her left shoulder raise-up with a casual shrug-off, you know that double message that says, it's ok but it's not? There was no time in her day to stand around giving me hell either. I knew where she was going after she finished with the ladder too, off to chop more firewood, feed the critters, cook more meals for half the town, spend time with her man, tend her flowers, run the post office, keep the peace among neighbors, and sit with her grandson. And that's just her morning schedule!

Mary handles so many jobs that were designed for men, or several men. She's been using one of those nasty chainsaws for many years and still has all her hands, fingers, feet, and toes and she's not sporting any gouges on her face from mishaps and hasn't been crushed by any falling trees, nor had her eyes poked out by any stabbing branches! Lucky, oh no luck had nary a thing to do with it. You can only be lucky with a chainsaw so many times before it catches up with you, unless you really know what you're doing and religiously follow a few safety rules. Even her dad cut off a few of his fingers on a buzz saw back when she was a kid so she wasn't going to make that mistake. Learn from your parents, I always say! Her motto: "If there's anything that needs doing that I can do without a man's help, I do it," she says, and she isn't kidding! We're not talking about light work either. She is just as apt to do the heavy work as a man would be. There's really not much she can't do. You'd have to follow her around every second of the day, day-in and day-out to catch her in a moment she couldn't handle and even if you did catch her laboring at something a bit difficult, she'd likely find some way to do it. It's a big deal to her to be able to do any job in front of her.

Ever since she was a little girl in Grande Prairie, Alberta, she knew how to handle a rifle, but in all her years she never once shot an animal with one. Not that she never tried to dispatch a Coyote or two now and then because they'd always be stealin' her Chickens. But the darn Coyotes never did show up at the right time. Whenever she loaded her rifle and set her mind to take a few of them out of this world, her timing was always off. She'd be sitting on a stump waiting for them to show up and they wouldn't, or she'd not show up and they would. Probably destiny, because she never was very big on the idea of killing them. They had to eat too! Even when she raised Cows and Pigs, someone else always did the shootin'. She'd help clean them afterwards but never did she raise a gun to one. That's not to say she didn't put and end to any critters. When something like that had to be done, to dispatch an old or sick Chicken, she did the deed herself. She states clearly that she never enjoyed killing anything but sometimes it has to be done. She really loves her collection of Pigeons but after a while there gets to be too many, so she dispatches a half dozen or so by catching them with a net and chopping their heads off. You probably wouldn't think of eating a Pigeon but that's the first thing that comes to her mind after doing something like that, not to waste the meat. She takes the bird's head and places it between two nails on a chopping block and brings the axe down on the neck. They flop around headless for a few seconds and its over. She dips them in pots of boiling water to loosen the follicles and the feathers pull right out. She harvests the parts of the bird that are good for eatin', like the breasts, then she cleans them thoroughly and either eats them that very evening or puts them in the freezer. You never know where her food is gonna end up either, usually in a spread of delectable dishes feedin' a hungry crowd some place or another.

The word 'can't' never creeps into Mary's vocabulary. If she ever hears you utter that foul word she stops in her tracks and looks at you, wondering what planet you're from. If there's something that needs to be done, she rolls her ideas over in her head for a bit then gathers up her tools and gets right down to whatever job needs to be done. A job is a job and what needs fixing or building gets fixed or built. She ain't waitin' around for a man to come along and do it. If one happens to be nearby, well he can just sit and watch for all she cares.

When asked how she builds things, and what tools she uses, she puts it plainly. "To make the dove house I used the same tools that anybody else would use, a hammer, saw, a few nails, and some Chicken wire. It's all still over there where I took it down. It's all underneath there," she said pointing to her back steps. "I had the dove house for roughly six, seven, or eight years. That was their summerhouse. In winter they were in my house for the first three or four years 'til I couldn't stand all their fuzz and dirt anymore. They make so much dust from fluttering around. I had them down in the barn for two or three years. I just got rid of them because, I loved them, I loved 'em, enjoyed their sounds and everything, just haven't got time for everything that's all there is to it!" she explained.

I asked what other things she built around the property. "I put a window in a cabin and put the fancy ends on the... what do you call that curly stuff on the end on the roof? I cut that out with a chainsaw. Old Bill's is still on there and it needs to get all stripped off. I cut a hole in the logs with a chainsaw and put the glass in for a window. That's a long time ago, probably eight or ten years. I built a couple of outhouses and I built the shed up at John's. John had so much stuff up there, bikes and a motor and stuff, and he had to have a place for it, so he said, Mary we gotta do something here, I need a little more room. So one winter I decided to build a shed for him and there it is, it's still there. John was the fellow that had the cabin on the hill there for ah... how many years, twenty some years! I put a little skylight thing in to let a little light in there. Just cut a hole in the gable end and I put fiberglass panels across it for light, and I put the door on. I always fix whatever needs to be fixed. A fence for the Deer, the Chickens, whatever you need to do, I do it! I built gates and fences, and a Gazebo out there. I had help with the Gazebo but basically I did all that work around the flower garden. I did that fence. I had a little help with the roof and corners but basically I did all the work myself. Fence panels, where you seen me diggin' yesterday! I did that all myself, every pillar and post there. I only did it so the Rabbits wouldn't get in, and they don't! I made a gate. I got two nails and pegged it with the two nails. I was in there the other day already and cleaned it up, you seen me! That's probably twenty or twenty-five years ago I built that. That's a Delphinium garden in there. I was born and raised on a farm and there are always things you hafta do. My mother, in fact I still have her hammer today, if there was something that needed to be fixed or done she would do it. Both my folks were very ambitious and hard working people and we grew up pickin' weeds in the crops. You didn't dare tramp on anything. You tramp between the rows, so those weeds didn't get into the wheat. Dad sold the wheat in the fall. If it had weeds in it your price would go down. We had Wheat, Barely, Alfalfa. When I say Alfalfa that's what dad made money on in the fall. You know a farmer never made a lot of money, I mean nobody ever did. But one fall dad made a lot of money with the Alfalfa crop and uh that's when he had extra money and he went back to Germany where he'd come from, for a holiday," said Mary.

Her mother's hammer is sixty years old, or older, yet it is in perfect shape and she uses it all the time. The quality of tools made today can't hold a candle to the quality back in those old times. She's had three chainsaws over the years. Her first one she recalled was a Husquavarna, her second one was a Johnsored, and her latest one is a Stihl 180.

She gave me a tour of some of the building projects she had undertaken over the years. As we began to walk she mentioned that a woman who supervises the tree planters in the area wanted to pasture her Horse in one of the animal enclosures. Most supervisors go around checking their tree planters on ATV's. This woman was doing it on horseback so Mary agreed to let her Horse stay on for a while in the Llama pen. As it turned out, it was a bonus for her grandson who was offered the benefit of a few riding lessons. She proudly displayed the shed she'd built and I could see the floor and framing were perfectly done. She made the fancy trim around the top for the shed as well as for any of her cabins on the property, for those that happened to need trim. It had been a winter project for her one year.

I complimented her on her workwomanship. "Sure there's nothing wrong with it at all. It's as good as any carpenter could do!" she said proudly. "A person could live in that shed!" I replied. "Well it's a little small!" she chuckled. "I'd actually considered living in something that small not too long before I came to live in your cabin!" I said. "Well, did you hear about that gal who is living in a tent in Williams Lake there? She had everything in the tent that she needed, even the Internet. She was a professional lady on top of it.

I don't know how long she's going to do it. Who knows, maybe they'll have an update on her story sometime," she replied. I figured probably half the population thinks that woman living in the tent is a few straws short a bale, and the other half think she's brave.

We walked over to the main house and up the stairs she'd built into the far end of the structure where her original fireplace room sat unused. Inside was a huge round rock fireplace with a metal hood that came up off the rocks and went up through the ceiling. Her son Robert built the hood in the center. Not bad for the woods! Coming off the wall to the left was a beautiful rock waterfall she built, and she pointed out that it contained some pretty Rodenite rock, a gift from her friend Frank Ayres. Ah, it had been many a year that room has sat unused but she didn't feel guilty because it took a lot of work to keep it going and the other end of the house now had a good wood stove that kept the whole place warm enough. "I'm startin' to get a little lazy, don't want to do some things anymore cuz I think I've done enough in life, I guess," she said. I suggested maybe she should kick back, maybe read more books, maybe go on over to her intellectual side. She paused and laughed, "I don't know if I have much interest in my intellectual side!"

We went back outside and she strolled me past her Rhubarb. "That's ready to eat!" she said pointing at the bushed-out leaves. She led me over to her Gazebo then stopped and pointed at the fenced-in garden she made. "Before I made this fence I had the garden enclosed with logs, five or six logs high. That was when we first came, and there was the garden inside. The logs heated up the ground earlier so it could be prepared and keep the cold off. They kept the wind off. They'd warm up during the day, and it was warmer. Then I took the logs down for firewood cuz you know you gotta make changes in life," she said.

In past years, by the time her annual barbeque and dance rolled around in the second week in July the Hops vines would usually be crawling twenty feet up around her windows and all around her house. A short and vigorous growing season is what you get here. Everything grows like it's on fire and then suddenly without warning it all dies off and the snow and ice descend. I asked, if people used the Gazebo during the dances to get out of the rain.

"Sixteen years I never had rain on a party! People used to joke about it. They'd say I'm going to Mary's party, ain't gonna be no rain! But the last time we had the party we had a big shower, yup!" she said. I wonder if maybe the rain was a sad ceremonial goodbye from the Gods now that the parties were coming to an end.

She went around showing me all the seedlings she started in the greenhouse. It was the end of May, summer was coming, and she always got a jump on her flowers. Many of them wintered in the house but there were the Annuals that she started each year. There were Pansies of every color, and Petunias, Geraniums, and Dusty Miller. She noted that nothing exists in the greenhouse over the winter months at forty below zero temperatures. "It freezes in there just like it does anywhere else!" she said

First Wilderness Auction

Mary organised the first local auction at her restaurant, Baxter's, and she raised four hundred dollars. She took a black Rabbit Baxter's had won the bid on, and let that critter run around in the restaurant. Good entertainment or good for eatin'. Something like that would be a crime in town.

She says that the greatest sadness in the world is that children are suffering and heir hunger and physical abuse really gets to her. "There shouldn't be a suffering child in the world. There are children suffering all over today!" she said. She started a campaign to collect funds for the Variety club Telethon and dreamed up creative ways to encourage even the most reclusive or miserly cowboy to donate a few coins to sick and under-privileged children. Instead of paying for their coffee at the restaurant she asked folks to drop a few cents into a can beside the cash register.

Once or twice, she auctioned off extravagantly wrapped mystery boxes. The final bid on one pretty box was said to have come in at seventy-five dollars. The highest bid came in at one hundred and ten dollars and the proud new owner excitedly set to unwrapping it to find out what he got. It was something no one expected, a great big block of ice, soon to become a big puddle of wet on the floor! Everyone roared themselves to tears, and from then on were quite suspicious, never knowing what they were gonna get. But that didn't stop any one of them from placing their bids because it was all for fun and mostly for the kids. That was just one example of Mary's sense of humour shining through, but also a testament to the fact that the act of giving is not bound in receiving materially. The real reward for the money spent is helping children.

In the year 2002 Mary helped make sure the dinner for the Anahim auction went off without a hitch and rallied her family together during the year leading up to the event to collect cash donations from each other in lieu of traditional birthday gifts. They collected two thousand five hundred dollars to purchase a Star-Walker, which was to be used to strengthen muscles and improve the co-ordination of crippled children, and her daughter Connie presented the donation at the Vancouver Telethon.

Mary has a way of pulling everyone around her together and has helped with the Variety Club Telethon for many years and she continues that tradition today. You can pick up any local newspaper or publication when some event is being reported, and there's Mary. She tries to be inconspicuous but anyone who knows of this legendary woman can spot her a mile off. You can't hide a face that beams the way hers does whenever she is workin' for others, especially children.

One fall, back in the early nineties, she decided to raise ten Turkeys for an October Turkey-shoot. She fed them so well that some accounts suggest at least one of them when dressed topped nearly fifty pounds. What she fed them was a mystery but whatever it was it was good. They put the Turkeys in a box with a hole cut in it so the Turkey could stick his head out. That's when the shootin' began. She raised about four hundred dollars that time. You could call her the Oprah of the wilderness. In fact she often says that she is ecstatically happy to have lived during Oprah-times. She tries never to miss an Oprah show, unless of course the TV signal is broken which happens sometimes and throws a damper on things. She clearly feels a kinship with Oprah and there's no doubt that they are both of the same heart. If Mary had been a rich woman there's no telling what she might have done, but you can be sure she would have set out on some sort of global program to do good, probably for children. She excitedly follows the adventures and good deeds of Oprah and I wonder what she would think if she knew how much she has inspired Mary!

The 2007 139-club telethon auction went even better than Mary hoped. At least 110 people showed up and the dinner and auction went on late into the evening. Now that's a ton of folks to cook for. There was a lot of chewing going on, all kinds of foods and desserts. She made her famous leafy-greens and potato salad recipes, buns, and cheesecake for everybody.

A good friend of Mary's, Len Lammoth, bought 100 draw tickets for a dollar each, for the prize of three Geese. Mary put in for 20 tickets. You'd buy draw tickets and put the names of people you don't like on the back or people who would not want to win the Geese. The idea was all in fun. So Len bought his tickets for Merrit Sager who had no use for any Geese. Of course having a hundred draw tickets with his name on the back insured that he who did not want the Geese, would win the Geese. Katherine went up to him, smiled, and said, "Mary wants the Geese!" His immediate response was, "There is a God!" Maybe Len secretly knew that Mary would somehow end up with the Geese no matter who won but it all turned out well for everyone. Merrit didn't have to take the Geese home but that wasn't the end of it. Someone got the bright idea that a little more money could be made off these Geese for the Variety Club Telethon. So they re-auctioned them off! Ken Thompson got the Geese the second time but he didn't want them either, so Ken gave them back to Bernie who had been looking after them. Then Bernie gave them to Mary. When she got them home she put all but one in the pen with the one she already had but one refused to go in. She chased him around in the snow for a while but there was no way she could get him, so she decided to let him spend a few days outside by himself. He'd either get lonesome for the other Geese or he'd be eaten by some marauding critter. That Goose stood at the fence looking in, yacking at the others for a few days. One morning Mary and Connie were down at the barn with determined faces and finally managed to herd the Goose into the pen.

Killer Loons

The spine-tingling sound of Loons playing their vocal violins in the stillness of the wilderness, especially at night, is likened to hearing the harmonics of the universe itself. They are the strings of the sky's instrument. Could there be any question that Mary would love them? Every spring at least one pair of Loons touchdown in the Bay in front of her house and everyone knows that all wildlife is cherished but anyone who knows Mary also knows that the Loons hold a special place in her heart. She watches them swim, dip, dive, and glide along, crisscrossing in front of the window and pays special attention to where they choose to nest each year, then anxiously awaits the arrival of the little chicks. She keeps tabs on the nest and spends countless hours adoring them and pointing them out to friends and visitors as they paddle close to mom. She loves those little chicks to bits knowing full-well that not once in the more than thirty years the pair has been visiting have any of their chicks escaped the veracious appetite of the watchful circling Bald Eagles and the stealthy night Owls, who have their own chicks to feed. The first moment mama Loon puts any distance between her and her young they're goners. But Mary's end of the lake is set just like an ever-changing artist's canvass. All is beautiful, including nature's circle of life and death. Everything comes into being and has it's brief time in the sun, then goes out of being, back to the Earth, and so too go the baby Loon chicks. You know they're dead when she stops talking about them and gets on with admiring other little birds and critters that become a new episode in the living-painting of life.

She described how at least once she saw her beautiful Loons do something that most folks couldn't imagine Loons would do. One day while she was admiring them they disappeared beneath the water's surface, only to suddenly resurface across the Bay next to a clump of bobbing Ducks that were paddling in an area the Loons had claimed as their own territory. With the greatest of ease they snapped the necks of the unsuspecting Ducks. Who could have imagined that something as poetic as a Loon could be capable of such brutality? But what appears to be brutal to the Duck lover is just nature's way and seems to be devoid of guilt or conscience. We can't argue with it. Even the staunchest animal rights advocates are at a loss as to a solution. No amount of protest has ever been able to intervene in Mother Nature's determination. Her word is final, although at times she is so swift as to give the appearance of some form of compassion.

Record-high Mountain snow packs over the winter of 2006 caused major flood conditions in late May and early June around the entire province and Mary hadn't seen water levels on the lake rise so high, since 1976. Lars and Diane were a bit disappointed when she returned from her peddle-boat trip out to the small island where the Loons nest because she bore bad news. "The Loons have built their nest on a slope and it isn't sitting properly. Not a good sign. There are no eggs. Loons can't walk on land so they've gotta have their nests at the water. With the water levels so high it is unlikely they'll lay this time around. Oh well, nature has its cycles! Loons live for up to seventy years and mate for life. This pair is probably the very same one that has been coming here every year since I've been here," she said.

Bridle and Neuter for a Llama

It was the month of April and a mostly clear sunny day was upon the Chilcotin with a few light clouds passing by in the breeze. Mary was training her young Llama, Rachael, to accept a bridle. She was only a couple of months old and was rebelliously frisky behaving not much different than a Horse does when it's being broken in. She put the bridle over her head and let her sit with it on for a few hours then returned to the pen to try and catch her. But the Llama had so much room to run that she ended up chasing her around and getting nowhere. She finally resigned to letting her be alone for a while longer and would return again and again to the pen through the days ahead and work to get her to accept the rope going over her face. She didn't seem to be too impressed but Mary had seen it all before and knew she would calm down after a while. "You can't really sell a Llama if you can't bridle it," she said opening the gate on the pen. She went over to a big stack of fresh clean hay, a feast for a Llama I'm sure, and stabbed a pitchfork into the bale and hoisted a huge swath of straw over her shoulder and carried it to the main pen where many of her birds also roamed around. She spread the hay out on the ground and returned for another pitchfork load. Then she gathered a few eggs for baking and the next morning's breakfast into her shirt.

On June 27/2006 at about 2:30 in the afternoon I heard her calling me from outside my cabin. I had asked her to fetch me when the Llama shearer showed up to do a shave and clip for Harley the brown haired male, and Misty the white haired female. Mary ran over to tell me that the action was already underway and if I didn't really get a move-on I'd miss the whole thing. I barely had time to put on my shoes and she was already hoofing it back to the pen. "Wait fer me!" I yelled after her as I ran up the driveway. It took only a minute to get there but the shearing of the female was already half finished leaving one heck of a pile of beautifully fluffy wool on the ground. I felt like flopping down to sleep in the stuff.

As the shearer finished shaving Misty the white fur fell away like a blanket onto the dusty ground, revealing a thin wasted looking animal underneath. She'd gotten pretty thin using almost every ounce of energy to nurse her baby and of course fending off the continual advances of Harley the adult male who was ever ready to give her yet another infant to care for. She barely had time to recover from one pregnancy and delivery before Harley was all over her again. Mary had seen just about enough of that so after the male had been sheared she casually mentioned her plans to neuter him. The shearer said he performed about a hundred neuterings a year and could do the job right on the spot. Mary's face lit up! "If I'd have know that I'd have got ya to do him!" she replied. To her surprise he said, "Do you want me to catch him again and do him now? It only takes a minute or two!" Right quick Mary answered, "Oh yes, you could do that!" He nodded and headed for his tools. "Just let me check what I've got in the car!" he said as he rummaged around inside his glove box then popped his head up wielding a sharp thing. "I've got my Exacto knife, that'll work!" he said.

I was observing the shearing and clipping but I wasn't about to hang around for the neutering. It seemed rather crude to me. "Well, Mary I'll be seeing ya," I said squeamishly. The shearer looked up and waved his rather crude tool in the air. "I could use a spoon but this'll work better, it's nice and sharp," he said confidently. Needless to say, neither the spoon nor the Exacto knife appealed to my sensibilities and I was gonna go missing for that action. I felt my knees turn to rubber and nodded queasily increasing my stride toward my cabin and I had no eyes for lookin' back. But this is the way of the remote West. When a job has to be done you usually have two options. The first is to find the most basic method available to you, and the second option is not to do the job at all, and usually it's something that has to be done so you go with option number one, it's really that simple!

The next two mornings in this late June there came a frost. The temperature dipped to below zero the night before. It came as no surprise that the newly shaved Harley, minus his long wooly hair was a-shiverin'. If it hadn't have been cold outside one might have assumed he was shiverin' because he had to face the other Llamas without his manhood and wasn't relishing the prospect. I became aquainted with Mary's Llama in a most unusual way. Not long after I first arrived at the little log cabin in January 2006 I began making trips up to Mary's house to pick up eggs and chat a bit. I had to walk through the barnyard area to get to her house and while passing through I heard something running up behind me. I turned around quick to find Harley gaining on me at a full run. As he neared me I thought there was absolutely no doubt that he was going to crash into me, and flatten me out. I remember thinking there was no time, no place for me to go to get out of the way and there was just no way in the world, at the speed he was running that he had any time to stop. Not even if he wanted to, and judging by his speed it didn't appear he wanted to. I figured I was doomed. When he was about two feet away his feet simply came to a dead stop and a huge cloud of dust rose up around him and into my face. I had never seen an animal moving so fast, stop on a dime like that. He buried his nose in my hair and I realized right then that this Llama was severely interested in me. This Llama already had a girlfriend he'd fathered several offspring with, however his girlfriend was also as white as the coat I was wearing. I wondered if he was attracted to my coat. I tried to chalk it up to my imagination. I told my story to Mary when I saw her a few minutes later. She balked at the notion that her favorite Llama would behave in such a way toward a human. "Well I didn't make it up!" I said firmly. In all the years she'd had him he'd never showed any behaviors like that to anyone. There wasn't much I could do to convince her that he had the hots for me, at least not right then and there.

Some weeks later I was over sitting on Connie's porch chatting with her. This time I was wearing the kind of coat you don't mention to animal activists without riling them up. It was a cold morning and I had just washed my hair so I was a bit chilly. As I sat near the railing Harley walked up alongside and stuck his face between the cross boards and nuzzled his nose into my hair and began to preen me, running strands of hair through his teeth. After a few minutes of that I got up to leave, walked down the few steps

47

off the porch and turned to face Connie at the top of the stairs to say goodbye. Suddenly she sprang to her feet and yelled and grabbed her broom and started swingin' it as she rushed over to where, unbeknownst to me, he was rearing up behind me. I spun around in bewilderment to see what the commotion was about. Before I knew what happened, she told me. "He would have broken your back!" she said in shock. I laughed and told her about how he had approached me before and that I didn't think Mary believed me. Connie was my witness and bore the truth to Mary.

The next day Harley was locked up in his pen and wasn't allowed out. He paced back and forth along the length of the enclosure as I passed through the hobby farm to get back to my cabin from yet another visit to Mary's house for something. Obviously he was itching to get out and not too pleased with me. I knew why the Llama was locked up. It was to calm my fears that Harley might attack me. I was quite nervous about the whole thing. Being run-at by a huge Llama is a bit unnerving. I felt a bit relieved but a bit guilty that he was hemmed in like that. As it turned out Harley agreed I should feel bad. His body language told me that he knew exactly why he was locked up, and I was to blame. He would have nothing to do with me and when I approached the enclosure to try and pet him through the gate he snubbed me, turning his head away and pointed his nose to the sky. I tried to follow him along the fence to coax him into friendship but he showed his teeth and snorted, always pointing his head away to show he had no further interest in me, not a happy Llama at all. After a short while he was allowed to roam free again but he always took a wide berth when we had to cross paths and snubbed me completely for at least a full year. Although he wouldn't have anything to do with me he carefully screened my cabin visitors. Any men coming through had to get past him first. Occasionally he would become aggressive if he saw a man within twenty feet of me. He'd approach and make all kinds of vocal threats and stamp his feet and kick up dirt like a Bull protecting his harem. I found it a bit odd that he wouldn't go anywhere near me, yet displayed a definite sense of protection over me. I had no idea what to make of it. Finally, Harley and I established boundaries and now he allows me to pet him but only occasionally, playing very hard to get.

Foxes and a Baby Llama

An injured Fox had begun to hang around Mary's Chicken barn, sizing up the Chickens and Geese. How she got injured is up for debate, a trap, or maybe a scrap with some other formidable critter, nobody knows. But the blood she dripped in the snow as she hobbled off into the tree line after coming from the direction of the Chicken barn, might have been a result of a botched attempt on the Chickens. One of the Llamas may have given her a swift kick. After the wild dogs killed all Mary's Deer, the Llamas didn't take too kindly to anything remotely canine on their property. You go sniffing around a Chicken barn for a meal you takes your chances! She was a pretty Fox too, with orange underneath and a mix of charcoal, grey, and white on top.

A month after the first sighting, Mary saw the same limping Fox again, hobbling up the driveway away from the barn. She must have been down there for an hour or more, judging by the number of tracks she left in the snow. Mary found them all over the place, circling the barn a number of times, zigzagging around the fences, up and down the driveway. But, there were no Chickens missing, so she couldn't have been having too much success. But, Mary knew when to lock everything up. At times like these, the birds go to jail until the danger has passed or has at least been reduced. You never know when a wild animal is going to set his sights on the barn, so all you can really do is keep a watchful eye out, and take necessary steps once you've identified a threat. You're bound to lose some barn critters once in a while.

This Fox eventually set up a few good perching spots nearby, creating a good line of sight that would enable her to snatch a Chicken. She probably would have moved in and picked some off sooner than she did if it hadn't been for those Llamas. They mix tightly with the birds around the barn and could be quite a handful if you peeve them off. She probably watched the Llama's habits and times they came and went from the barn throughout the days and evenings to calculate her plan of attack. They didn't come up with the term "sly as a Fox" for no reason. Eventually she did come up with a strategy for a quick way in and out of the Chicken coop. Although at first, Mary wondered if maybe it wasn't the Fisher that stole a Chicken and ate it under her house. She'd found the remains under there. But then she decided it was probably the Fox because she'd seen her around for sure, but she hadn't seen the Fisher at all.

It wasn't long before all doubt as to the identity of this latest assassin was pinpointed, when one day Mary saw the Fox go up and over the Chicken fence like it wasn't even there. She was pretty good at it too, like she'd been doin' it for a while.

The 2007 return of Lars and Diane to Mary's Place in mid-May proved to be action-packed. They stayed in the cabin next to the Llama pen because they love to be around the Chickens, Peacocks, and other personalities picking around in front of the cabin window in the mornings.

Mary let Lars name and bridle-train the new baby Llama. Every morning he would go out to the pen and wait 'til she rounded up the little guy he called Prince. He'd put the bridle and lead on, and spend hours calming him, walking him, and getting him accustomed to his brand new world.

Diane would often come into the pen and offer handfuls of sweet clover and when Lars took him for walks she'd trail along behind picking tiny wild purple and white Jacob's Ladder blossoms for the kitchen table. They couldn't believe it when Mary told them there was a red mama Fox and two Fox Kits denned-up under a nearby cabin. The babies were obviously fathered by the gray Fox also seen lingering around over the winter.

The mama would go off hunting for long stretches. While she was gone the two little Fox Kits poked their heads out into the morning sun and inched cautiously outside, and romped around in the dust.

As most babies do, they were soon ready for a nap and plopped on top of each other and fell asleep.

Lars and Diane laughed when Mary told them that the mama Fox had been stealing her Chickens and took every last one of her Rabbits, even a pregnant one, which really upset her. That Rabbit had just been given to her to look after for the very purpose of avoiding Foxes in the first place. Mary didn't know what she was gonna tell her friend!

A solution would soon have to be found to the Fox/Chicken dilemma, otherwise within a few short months the entire Fox family would be raiding the Chicken barn. The mom was really starting to cut into Mary's egg supply too. Just one Fox can devour a Chicken a day. As cute and cuddly looking as they were the Red Fox, the Gray Fox, and now two babies, simply could not be allowed to stand! They were unacceptable tenants.

One late morning when Lars and Diane were going into the pen for the Llama, Mary was standing with them and she noticed the little Fox Kits had emerged from the den. She snuck up around the back of the old uninhabited log building and crept along the sidewall and peered around the corner. They didn't notice her standing just a few feet away. Although she knew she'd have to thwart this situation quickly, she didn't want to kill the poor things. "They're just like bums sleeping in the superstore!" laughed Lars. "Or a jewel-thief sleeping under the counter at the jewelery store!" added Diane.

Mary defaulted to Logan who set to figuring a plan on how to out-fox those Foxes. They decided to collect those babies to discourage the mom from denning there next year. He first tried standing at the entrance with a fishnet in his hand, in hopes of grabbing them when they came out to play. There would be several days at a time that the Foxes didn't come out of the hole, so standing there with a net endlessly seemed useless.

Then he decided to try a live trap, so he caged off the base of the building so the mama Fox was locked out and placed the trap inside the enclosure. It wasn't long before one of the Kits curiously peeked out and walked right into the trap, lured by the aroma of a few greasy beef and pork smokies.

After he nabbed him, he put him in a cage in the barn until Punky could come and get him. She was well known for her ability to look after wayward wildlife.

It took nearly a week to trap the second kit. I offered to raise him so he could be released back into the wild. After Logan caught him, he brought the little Fox kit down to my cabin. I handed him a small Dog collar, and he slipped it over his neck. Mary wanted no part of that. Collars on Foxes don't impress her at all and she shook her head and stood well back, refusing to help because she is totally against harnessing wildlife. As it turned out a Fox in a small cabin crying all night for his mother, and the strong musk in his poop was too much for me. So I regretfully sent the little infant back to Mary and she decided to send him on to Punky to be raised with the other Kit. So a call went out for her to come around and get him. It wouldn't have been long before he'd want to make a meal out of my little Dog and Mary's Chickens anyway. Mary raised her eyebrow. "You sure don't persevere very long, do you?" she said shaking her head at me. As I tossed my excuses around as to why I couldn't raise the little feller I could see none of it was washin' with her and I was a little embarrassed.

Mary crossed her fingers that the mama Fox would move on to another location now that her kits were gone. If she didn't, a re-evaluation of her fate would have to be considered. She simply could not afford to feed that Fox a Chicken a day anymore!

Monarch Icefield Tragedy

In April 1992 Mary and her wilderness home became the hospitality-hub for volunteers during the search for a missing young couple on the Monarch Icefields Bob Kovacs, a Canadian Armed Forces test pilot and former Search and Rescue pilot had recently married his beautiful young bride Jeni. They embarked on an alpine anniversary trek, carefully laying out a detailed map of their route, as well as indications of where they planned to be at given times along the way. They wore personal locator-beacons and did just about everything responsible hikers should do, so that in the event of an accident they could be found. They were competent hikers and seemed to have laid out their trip responsibly but as fate would have it, they did not return when they were scheduled to.

On April 27th a search team was dispatched and the helicopter crashed en-route to the area. One searcher was killed and nine others were injured. On May 5th the search was called off, some would say, before it even got started, apparently due to unsafe conditions.

Oddly, the search never resumed not even when the weather cleared. Although the couple took absolutely every precaution possible that would almost ensure they'd be found, the authorities did not even attempt to follow the clear details set out in the map. So Bob and Jeni Kovacs remained somewhere out there on the Monarchs and for months their personal locator beacons beeped away with no one to hear.

The authorities offered a very cold welcome to Mr and Mrs Cordona, Jeni's parents, when they arrived in the area. They were abruptly told, in no uncertain terms to turn around and go home, to give up. But no mother is going to do that, not knowing if her daughter was dead or alive. Mrs Cordona begged and pushed for the search to be resumed. She desperately wanted to find Jeni and bring her home, no matter what. But her pleading fell on deaf ears. There was no way on Earth that the official powers were going to be any help at all.

Local residents and pilots rallied together and formed their own search party. Mary's partner at the time, Nick, was the main driving force that motivated everyone to get out there and get to the bottom of things. And once again Mary came through for folks in need and acted as the quiet root system holding things together, providing cabins to the volunteer searchers and family members of the missing kids. She fed everyone and made them feel that someone cared. She felt very bad for Mr. and Mrs. Cordona, who had traveled across the country to find their girl, and were treated so poorly.

One of the local pilots, Frank Cherne, a friend of Mary's, rigged-up a little receiver to pick up Bob and Jeni's locator beacon signals, and the search was on. This volunteerism seemed to rub law-enforcement and the military the wrong way and a very odd situation developed. Being that one of the missing persons was a Canadian Forces test-pilot and former Search and Rescue pilot, you'd think there'd have been a little more action undertaken to bring home one of their own. But it seemed every roadblock possible was at hand.

The volunteer pilots spotted the tent of the missing pair several months later in the snow at an altitude of eight thousand feet.

Sometime later another volunteer pilot was on a flight and decided to swing around and take a look in an area the couple was thought not to have ventured into, and he found the pair. Jeni's face, upper torso, and arms were exposed resting on the pristine snow and Bob's head was resting in her lap. It was said that Jeni was found frozen, perfectly preserved, and that she was still as beautiful as she had been in life. They must have fallen holding each other because there wasn't a flake of snow between them. She may have survived for a while and dug her arms out, because they were resting on top of the snow along with her ice axe. It appeared that they had been caught in an avalanche after negotiating an unexpected storm along their route and venturing farther off their plotted path than they intended. This may have been what took their lives.

It seemed that the tragedy was not over yet. The Cordona family argued with the authorities about who would recover the bodies. Mrs. Cordona didn't want the government involved. She saw no reason for them to take credit now when all along they hadn't lifted a finger to help search, and in fact in many instances had tried to stall any efforts made by anyone who did. She wanted the volunteers to extricate her daughter so things got heated and the government wanted to prevail. The 'powers' had been embarrassed enough that they weren't the ones who found them, and probably didn't want to have the volunteers show-them-up any more than they already had.

Jeni's mother Winnie stood and watched as their frozen bodies were chopped from the ice and lifted by helicopter net and carried to the Nusatsum picnic grounds at Odegaard falls, the spot where their fateful trek initially began.

As things wound down after the ordeal and Mary's Place began to return to normal, the gratitude came pouring in. Mary didn't want anyone to make a fuss but they did! The dead couple's family had bonded with the volunteers and Mary was at the top of that list. Cards and letters filled with words of love and appreciation poured in. Without Mary's partner Nick, pushing for things to get done, and without her holding down the fort, feeding and sheltering everyone, Jeni and Bob would still be out there lost in those mountains to this very day.

Interestingly, some media accounts suggest that Bob and Jeni were found in a crevasse. This would certainly make it more difficult to locate them from the air, giving the government an excuse for not finding them. However, upon interviewing some of those who were at the scene, it was said that they were not in a crevasse but that they were out in the open, which starkly contradicts the official story!

Frank and Claudia Cherne recalled some of the details of the events that surrounded the tragedy.

"I was one of the people flying, searching for the couple. The parents came out. They wanted someone to go and look for the kids. Part of the time they stayed in Bella Coola," said Frank. "And that was when they did send a search party up there, what, in April?" said Claudia. "Right, that was when the accident happened. It was a regular search, then the helicopter went down," Frank added. "And that was when they said we can do nothing," said Claudia. "The parents stayed in Bella Coola for three months," said Frank. "They stayed trying to get someone to go and look and nobody down there would do anything," added Claudia. "Nick heard about it I guess through the highways or while he was traveling back and forth from Bella Coola. He organized a flight search one weekend," explained Frank. "But the parents didn't want to leave until they knew what had happened or they found the kids. They just persued it and persued it," said Claudia emotionally. "We met the family after searching. After we did the first flight, I was in one aircraft and Terry Brandt was in another. We found the tent pitched on the ice field up there. Jeni and Bob Kovacs left a map of their entire trek and this was on the furthest point of their trek up onto the Icefield. We found the tent there and Terry landed near it. I think he landed and looked at the tent but didn't persue it any further. At that time in June the tent wasn't covered by snow. It was out in the open. I'm sure it was covered when they originally searched. Then the RCMP was notified and they went up there with their helicopter and found that indeed it was their tent. And there was a lot of their undeveloped film there, and a map of where they were gonna go the next day. They were going to go three points. One was up to... I don't remember the name of the mountain, Mount Dagon. And they were going to go to the top of that and then cross-country ski back to their camp. Well Terry in his plane and I in mine, we both noticed that there were some unusual markings on the snowfield, and what it ended up being was the tracks of their cross-country skis compressed into the ice. Eventually, almost a month later Rob Owens was in the area with his helicopter. He flew up around the area just to see if he could see something. This was the end of July, first part of August. He flew around the area where the glacier breaks away at the top. Jeni's upper torso was visible when Rob flew over," explained Frank. When asked to clarify if they thought Jeni was in a crevasse or not, "No, no, they were actually buried by the avalanche," said Claudia. "She was not in the crevasse! There had just been an avalanche down the face and she was just on the ice!" said Frank. "And they were both buried upright. I think it broke his back," said Claudia shaking her head solemnly. "They were both together anyway, and her upper part of her torso was out of the snow," added Frank. "They were holding hands! I think so!" said Claudia. "In any event, they were together. A professional climber came in to try and extricate the bodies. Between him and the authorities there was some disagreement as to who would do the extrication," said Frank. "After everything was found, it became very political. They (the authorities) didn't want anyone else around. They were the ones that had given up and weren't going to go back in," said Claudia.

There are many news accounts of this tragedy. One newspaper article displays a photograph of the helicopter pilot who found the bodies holding the many pages of Bob and Jeni's detailed journals. The story also gained some attention from at least one high profile movie star, the late Christopher Reeve. He agreed to star in a movie about Bob and Jeni's trip, but then he had his tragic horseback riding accident and that was the end of that movie, at least for now. Mary doesn't talk too much about those sad times, although she does keep a special album full of articles, cards, and letters of thanks for bringing folks together to resolve a tragedy.

World Champ Mighty Mike

"Mike Kadar bought a piece of land from me and built his house there in 1987 or 88. He rented for the first half a year or so, then he bought one of my lots, cuz I had three or four for sale. He bought one of them and built the house where Connie is now, the house with all the rockwork. He lived there until, well how long has he been gone now, five or six years! He was probably in his late twenties or early thirties when he was here. He was here for ten or twelve years. He worked at the mill and did odd jobs for everybody.

He'd been arm wrestling before he came here. I think he'd already won one World Championship before he came and then he was still arm wrestling and he'd go to all these competitions. He had the BC one. There was the American one. Then there was always the World Championship. He'd go over and do arm wrestling. He won the world championship several times. He and Nick went to Russia. I don't remember exactly what year but…the late eighties or…you see I gave all that information to him so I don't know. I've got a couple souvenirs. He won the one in Russia when they went. I know he won the one in Sweden …the world championship. And he went to Israel.

There was nobody to help him so we had several dances, fundraising dances, to make money for him to get to the championships. His parents really didn't have anything to help him with and so it was a community effort to raise the airfare. And I had T-shirts made and all that. Claudia might have one. Somebody recently had one of those T-shirts but I forget who that was," explained Mary.

I asked if Mike arm-wrestled pretty much everyone in town. "Yeah he did some of that too. He had an arm wrestling stand set up just over here right at his house, a special table and chairs. Everybody lost to him most of the time I imagine.

Bill Bremmeyer took us one time to the North American competition out of Edmonton, Wetaskwin Alberta. He won that one too! I think he got wore out after a while because after you win the world championships two or three times, you know, what else is there? I got a whole photo album made up for him but I gave it all to him.

Any time I needed help he was right here to help me out. All the time he did all kinds of jobs around here, I can tell you that. He was always helping me out! It was all physical work. He did cement work, the Deer house, Chicken house, all that cement work, he did. Fences, anything, gates, anything I couldn't fix he would fix for me. One day I see him coming back," she said.

As things would be, there wasn't really any prize money to be had for all the titles Mike won. You'd really have to love the sport to travel halfway around the world for a competition and come home without a purse. And the folks who make it personal enough that they are willing to fundraise for you to compete around the world, have to really believe in you. Not all winnings make you rich or bring product-endorsement contracts to your door.

When Mike moved away he gave Mary his Pigs, which he'd always kept at his house. She put them in her Chicken pen for a while until she could figure out where to put them. Two fellas came with a truck and began to herd this one Pig into the back. When the men cornered him, he didn't oink, squeal, or snort, he started barking like a Dog. Everyone stopped when they heard it. He must have learned how to bark from Mike's Dog. That Pig just sat there barking as if to be speaking his last rites, which probably didn't buy him much more than a few minutes. After the barking they just hauled him off, probably not to join a circus act either.

Stompin' the Night Away

The annual Rodeo at Anahim Lake was, and still is, a boom-time for the Chilcotin, which crawls with visitors from everywhere. The local resorts and lodges are completely booked with spectators as well as participants who follow the circuit. They feel at home here because if you're a cowboy or cowgirl your hat and boots are worn authentically.

For ten years or more Mary worked the gates, taking admission tickets and sometimes cooking. One year she cooked 720 hamburgers. "I went home afterwards looking like a grease ball and decided there'd be no more of that!" she explained.

One year, during the second week in July of 1982, the weekend after the Rodeo, she decided to throw a party for her neighbor Mr. Lemke, a potluck for his 80th birthday. She carried out the planning with her particular brand of style, organizing, cooking, and setting up picnic tables all around the grounds in front of her house. She brought in a live band, enlisted a few helpers, and built a dance floor. One hundred of the town's-folk showed up at the shindig with dishes of food and birthday wishes for Mr Lemke so there was a wide range of tantalizing aromas wafting from the various recipes, and the wide selection of colorful salad dishes welcomed the eyes. The partiers stuffed themselves, burped, indulged in a spirit or two, and danced their faces off.

Music from the live band echoed down the lake, past the Loons, tweeked the ears of a few Coyotes, quivered the odd blade of grass and penetrated the wilderness night which had never heard the word 'city'. They danced and laughed till the wee hours. And when it was assured that Mr Lemke's birthday had been done-proud and not even a die-hard hanger's-on could dance another step or eat another morsel, folks headed home already looking forward to next year's shindig.

Mary and her help-entourage cleaned up and disassembled the dance floor right after and she loved every bit of the job too. If one of her helpers had to leave early, she paid it no never mind and just went ahead and picked up the slack. She hadn't realized it yet but she'd started a new tradition that would continue for the next sixteen years.

Mr Lemke died two years later at the age of eighty-two but every year one week after the Rodeo, Mary would have another shindig. You could say that the tradition became a semi-permanent tribute to Mary's neighbor.

It wasn't long before the folks showing up at these barbeque-dances numbered three hundred and fifty, and it required one hundred and fifty pounds of meat to feed 'em. There'd be pork, beef, or turkey... and there was always fish. Wild Rainbow Trout smoked with Poplar wood is particularly delicious and one of mother natures alternatives to candy. Lyman Thompson did all the meat cookin' over an open barbeque pit.

Most often it was Mary who initiated local events, and if she didn't start something she was most often the one in the background organizing and holding things together, always doing the cooking.

Frank and Betty Ayers have known her for a lot of years and reminisced from their kitchen table one afternoon during the summer of 2006, especially about the barbeque-dances she hosted. Frank recalls the road into Mary's Place. You can still see remnants of her road, which is actually nothing short of a 4-km long driveway leading in from highway 20. "Sometimes you couldn't get out for months unless you walked in grueling Loon-shit (mud)," said Frank Ayers. Even today you can still see the remnants of the old trail into Mary's Place alongside the new gravel road.

Like many other folks these two longtime friends recall how she always baked donuts, bread, and buns and how she bought commercial equipment to make everything. They remember the wholesome milk from her Cows and the delicious eggs and fondly recall her dances.

"She'd asked everyone to bring a dish of food. We had enough meat for three hundred people, Beef, Lamb, Salmon, or whatever meat folks brought in," said Betty. "We'd wrap it up in burlap and wire it together then cook it over an open fire, lakeside. Lyman Thompson, a rancher from Kleena Kleene brought in a chuck wagon with a canvas hoop over it and made big pots of coffee over the fire-pit. They always kept the beer and soda-pop cool by bringing in a canoe or some sort of boat and filling it with ice. But there wasn't too much soda pop in the boat, mostly beer which was free of charge because there were often three or four kegs left over from the Anahim Rodeo the week before," said Frank.

Folks would be whooping it up on the stage in their dancin' boots and one of the favorite songs was 'Margaritaville'. Mary's partner, Nick, was singin' and playing rhythm guitar. As Frank was plucking away on his, he was helpless to do anything when a drunken cowboy riding a Horse rode up onto the stage and stepped down onto the hood of his 1966 Ford pickup truck and crunched it with his cowboy boots. "The guy didn't see much wrong with what he'd done," said Frank.

Eventually, Mary's annual dances had to come to an end. Too many uninvited young kids were showing up, coming all the way from Williams Lake looking for a party and free beer. Considering the number of invited folks already attending, the whole idea became unmanageable with young kids getting behind the wheel of a car and driving that wretched highway just to get drunk. She refused to have any hand in young kids driving drunk. It was too much of an enticement and a bad situation was in the making so she called it quits.

Frank and Betty recalled Mary's Variety-Club auctions for sick children and her notorious block-of-ice mystery-box. "Tony Backmine paid fifty dollars for the first one and no one ever forgot it, and that was twenty five years ago," said Frank.

They recalled Mary's Coyote problems and how they'd always come after her Ducks and Geese. She couldn't manage to catch the Coyotes so her partner, Nick, devised a method to try and take care of that nuisance once and for all. "Nick tied one end of a string around a bedroom dresser drawer and the other end around some sort of carcass. The idea was that when the Coyote yanked on the meat it would pull on the dresser drawer and that would wake everyone up. Then they were gonna go out and shoot the Coyote," said Frank. But however smart the idea seemed to be, in the end all that happened was they ended up sleeping through the night only to wake up the next day and find the dresser drawer on the floor and the Coyote had made his usual escape.

Frank recalled how at one time there were two Bats hanging behind Mary's stereo speakers in the corner of the living room. Nick was not gonna let this one get away so he pulled out his 22-Calibre rifle and pointed the barrel up behind the speakers and let go some shots. "Those bullet holes are still in the wall to this very day," laughed Mary.

Founding the BC Floatplane Association

The last year Mary had her post-rodeo barbeque dance party for Mr. Lemke was the first year the BC Floatplane Association was started at Nimpo Lake. It was formed by a group of about eight people, one of which was Mary's partner.

"Nick sort of put it together," said Claudia Cherne. "Nick was charged with landing on one of the Turner Lake chains. The Parks gave him either a warning or a citation or whatever for landing on one of the lakes there. And of course the final result was they didn't have the authority to do anything as long as you're landing in a body of water and not getting out onto the shore," recalled Frank. "They were closing a lot of the lakes and things in the area. They were only going to have it open for hikers and horseback riders" said Claudia. "And commercial outfitters," added Frank. "Yeah and they were excluding, you know, planes flying in. The point that they were trying to bring across or the reason the association was formed was the fact that all of these other things leave marks on the land itself! Where a floatplane flies in, they do no damage to the area!" said Claudia. "Now, through the efforts of the Floatplane Association and Parks we have a very good rapore. We've gone out and done a lot of cleanups. This last year we went out and installed signs on the trail up to Hunlin Falls at the overlook," said Frank. "Well, and every year they have a project," said Claudia. "Oh one year at Widgeon Lake we built the outhouses and one year we went up to Nalooza and cleaned up about twelve truckloads of garbage people had left up there," recalled Frank. "Oh that was terrible, the mess!" added Claudia. "Usually we go up on a

Saturday and then on Sunday the members of the Association volunteer to do a fly out. There were about twelve people. Mary hosts and provides, well between her and the other gals in the area they provide the entertainment and food for Saturday night for the Floatplane Association members," said Frank.

Horsepack Trips

"See, Mary was raised around Horses, so she tried having Horses here for the guests and things like that. It was just too much work with all the other things she does. But she does love riding when she has the opportunity, so here again she would get a group of people together to go on a Horse pack trip, and she would organize it all," explained Claudia. "It would be at the time of year when all the wild flowers would be at their peak!" said Frank. Then both Frank and Claudia rang out together, "At the end of July."

"In order to cut down on expenses Mary would volunteer and do the cooking and us girls would help. But anyway, onetime everybody slept on a foamy inside the tents. Well she got permission from the trip guides, Roger and Wanda, and brought her little folding cot because the packhorses had to pack it and everything. There was a wind that came up that day while we were out riding. When she came back her tent wasn't there. And she let-out with this holler, it was so funny! "Where's my tent!" Like somebody took her tent! So we looked down over the hill and it just rolled down the hill. Anyway the fellas went down and got the tent for her and brought it back up," laughed Claudia. "I think your first time, your first trip you had a Horse that was thirty some-odd-years old. It was one of Lester Dorsey's Horses," said Frank. "That was the second trip" replied Claudia. "Oh ok, I don't know which trip! I thought it was the first trip," he said defaulting to her memory being that she was the one who rode the Horse. "We'd have a certain ice chest where we'd put the food and we had all of the cooking utensils," she said. "We had the iron-grill that went over the fire and crank-up there. Our guides, Roger and Wanda were well set up for pack-trips. They had all the kitchen stuff. They had stations setup along the route where they'd tie the Horses and cook meals," said Frank. "Remember that time when we were up on top of the mountain, we had sleet, oh my, she was so cold that time! Remember she went and sat down by the bush, and we had stopped, and were overlooking the valley down there where there were a lot of Caribou," said Claudia. "Overlooking Pan Valley, yeah!" replied Frank. "Yah and it was cold enough, there was sort of a hail, and the Horses just stopped until the storm got through. But it was cold. The wind was blowing!" recalled Claudia vividly. "One time along the way, up through Cork-Screw Basin between the Itchas and the Ulkatcho we stopped at a little cabin next to a lake and caught some fish. There's a little old wagon trail that goes up through Corkscrew Creek we often take. One time we ran into a couple of Parks Biologists. I remember the two gals that were up there studying the Caribou. But I think that was the third trip. We ran into them at one of the camps, but for the most part we didn't see anybody. The first trip we took we went out for six nights, seven days, yeah!" said Frank.

Anyone who knows Mary also knows that flowers are a big part of her everyday life and she particularly loves the alpine wild flowers she sees on her horseback riding trips. Fireweed (which is stunted in alpine areas), Paintbrush, Lupins, white Daisies, pink and white Heather, cream and light-brown Anemones, and mauve Mountain Aster. "The last trip we went on, she wanted to go up and see the flowers at this one particular place because the first time we went up there it was just so beautiful. Mary's got pictures where she's just sitting in this sea of wildflowers. I walked up this incline cuz it felt good to just walk. I walked up there and all of a sudden it opened up around this corner into this big field of flowers and I called back to Frank. I told him, I says, bring your camera! So he came up and oh... so then everybody came up and was taking pictures. It was just gorgeous!" said Claudia gasping with excitement as she recalled the day. "So the last trip, Mary wanted to go up and see if the flowers were just as beautiful and that was the year she twisted her back just the day before we left. But she wanted to go anyway to see the flowers. But she got so bad she couldn't ride. All she could do was walk! So finally we took a vote and called a helicopter. They came in and picked her up. Next day we were going to go look at the flowers without Mary, and the flowers... they just weren't there! So she didn't miss anything. That was the first thing she asked when we got back from the trip. "How were the flowers?" We had to tell her she didn't miss anything! They just weren't that pretty!" said Claudia.

"So, we'd ride for the day and then we'd camp," said Claudia. "When we went for six or seven days there'd be two spots where we'd camp and leave the camp for a day. And we had the same camp for two days. Just take a day ride out! But most of the time we packed up camp everyday and setup camp every evening when we stopped.

Roger and Wanda knew how to pack a Horse and had scales to make sure the packs were the same weight on both sides. You had to know how to attach the pack-boxes to the pack-frames, how to tie everything on so it'd stay put," explained Frank. "Usually the Horseflies would get to bothering the Horses so bad, so about three days before the end of the trip they had this stuff that they'd rub the Horses down with," said Claudia. "Deet!" replied Frank. "To protect the Horses cuz the Horseflies would make these big sores," she added. "Roger and Wanda did a really good job of taking care of their Horses, keeping them in good condition, maintaining them on the trip.

One time Roger saw the tail end of a Bear as it was going away, and a couple of times we stopped and spent a few hours watching herds of Caribou. One time we watched a pair of Wolves for a while on the other side of a valley in the Itchas," said Frank. "Oh yeah, that was neat!" said Claudia. "Yeah, that was!" he added.

Horsefly Races

Frank and Claudia Cherne remembered how they indulged in a little Horsefly racing when they stopped for lunch at Corkscrew creek.

"Roger brought up the subject of the Horsefly races and showed us how to load the Horsefly. Well, it takes two people. You have to work as a team. First of all you catch a Horsefly. You go around the Horses and the Horseflies were just driving them nuts that day. You catch one and you carefully hold him so you don't squish him with the rear of the Horsefly out where the other person can pull the last little bit of the rear of the Horsefly off. That leaves a real sticky little glob there. You take a little piece of toilet paper or Kleenex and tear it to about a half-inch, a long streamer of paper. Then you twist the end of it into a point. You push that into the rear of the Horsefly and it sticks there. When you release the Horsefly it flies like an airplane pulling a banner with this long streamer. Sometimes they'll go a couple hundred yards before they land somewhere. Sometimes they'll get up and fly outta sight. You let 'em go one at a time and watch to see who's fly goes the farthest before it lands. It was something to pass the time in the afternoon when we were taking a break, a way to get rid of a few more Horseflies that were buggin' the Horses. Everyone was laughin' so hard, it was just sort of hilarious. I've seen one towing a piece about eighteen inches to two feet long. Some of 'em would take off and fly a big distance or around in circles. They all went pretty far," laughed Frank.

Mary and her groups went off for quite a few Horse trips into the rugged Itcha and Ilgachus mountain ranges, but Frank and Claudia haven't made it to the Rainbows yet but they do have an eye toward doing it sometime. They've got Rainbow Mountains on the brain and their eyes light up at just the mention of another trip. Frank notes that the Rainbows are not part of Roger and Wanda's territory and that they'd be going with new guides. When friends are important to you, as is true with Mary's group, even switching guides must be a sad good-bye to old friends.

Oh, the Poor Deer

Mary had a hankering for trying new things so she decided to try her hand at raising domestic Deer. She purchased a half dozen pregnant females and worked tirelessly from sun-up to sun down constructing a Deer pen. Neighbors helped a bit with the construction, digging holes and putting up Chilcotin Pine Poles. She strung a mesh fence and finally after the last post was pounded in and the last wire was strung and tied, she excitedly encouraged her timid Deer into the pen, five Does, and one Buck. All the Does were said to be pregnant but you just couldn't tell so it was a waiting game to find out how many would be born.

The slightest sound or sudden movement sent them springing-off in unison, bounding down to the waterfront into some low-lying Willows where they hid for a long time. They'd peek out from behind the bushes, one eye at a time and delicately step out into the open, always extremely cautious. Their natural instincts never leave them.

With the greatest amount of patience Mary warmed up to them by calling ever so softly, cooing in her gentlest voice, stepping forward slowly offering the sweetest treats she could find from the surrounding landscape, such delights as sweet clover, sugary-sweet apples, and freshly-ground oats. She laid them down on the ground and quietly backed away, letting them munch in peace.

Little by little, after weeks of cooing and bearing sweet gifts she was able to get a bit closer and managed to create a bond with the head-Deer who ventured over and nuzzled his furry nose and lips into her hand and ate a bit of sweet-clover. It took a couple of months for the rest of the Doe's to warm up to Mary, before she was able to come and go freely and the Deer began to love her.

This Human-to-Deer bond became a very important thing in her life and she adored them, and they adored her.

One morning she glanced over at the pen and unexpectedly saw the pangs of birth in action. Her babies were now being born. The fawns were immediately tame and instinctively took to her mothering. She had no idea how dearly she would come to love those little spotted fawns.

At one point she managed to end-up with fourteen Deer and she knew this was simply too many! So she did what she had to do and butchered seven, and put them in the freezer. Like a lot of other unpleasant things that are the trademark of a wilderness life, it had to be done!

The remaining Deer became her babies and she let them roam around and socialize with the resort guests. But eventually wildlife officers told her to put them back in the pen so they wouldn't breed with the wild Deer roaming the land, so she sadly complied!

One early morning in June, around 4:30 AM the Llama she named Harley woke her with a terrible screeching. She heard Dogs barking and a whole lot of commotion and knew something was wrong. She picked up her flashlight and ran out into the darkness and grabbed a pitchfork and ran down to the Deer pen but could see, nor hear any disturbance. Suddenly she spotted two Shepherd-like Dogs (one black one, and one black and gray one) making their escape from inside the pen. She watched them go up one side of the fence and down the other, like it was a ladder. Harley seemed to have calmed down so Mary concluded that she had interrupted the Dogs before they could do any damage. She saw no Deer around so she concluded that they must have jumped the fence to get away from the Dogs and she would go round them in the morning, which was only a couple of hours away. A false sense of security came over her as she chalked-up the racket to having probably been the two wild Dogs just paying a visit to the Chicken barn, and went back to bed.

But all was not well in the barnyard. When she went to the barn to give them their morning treats there was blood splashed throughout the Deer pen and she knew what really happened the night before. The bodies of four of her pet Deer lay dead on the ground, their throats ripped open, faces torn apart, with holes in their stomachs, just viciously slaughtered. The Dogs had managed to climb right up over the fence and down into the Deer pen. They stalked and quietly killed all but one of her pet Deer and not one of them had uttered a single cry. Only one shaking, wide-eyed, terrified Deer stood standing amidst the carnage. How this one helpless Deer escaped death that night was a mystery.

She soon found out that it was much worse than she could ever have imagined because she also found blood spattered throughout the Chicken barn and eighteen of her egg-laying Chickens lay stone cold dead. The dogs had a hay-day; five Deer and eighteen Chickens slaughtered. Mary and Logan, along with the help of a neighbor loaded the Deer into the back of her pickup truck and drove them into the bush where she offered their flesh back to the wild as life sustaining food for Bears and Wolves, continuing the cycle of life. She loaded up all her dead Chickens and took them to the landfill.

Two months later, during the month of August, the final chapter of this tragic event unfolded. Mary's daughter Connie was visiting and was sitting on the porch of one of the old cabins next to the Deer pen and a terrible scream broke the silence of the absolutely still wilderness night. It was Harley the Llama screeching again. Connie set into action, and ran to fetch her mom and they raced back down to the Deer pen with their flashlights toward a flopping sound. What they saw was a nightmare, Mary's last Deer on the ground thrashing in a mud hole, blood gushing from his open throat, flank, and back with each death-throw. Connie knew there was no way to get a hold of the thrashing Deer in the dark and suggested they let him alone and look in the morning.

The light of the next day revealed the gruesome horror of the night before. Her Deer was still in the mud-hole but his eyes stared blankly up at the sky. There lay Mary's cold, stiff, lifeless Deer. He was gone! When they went into the muck to remove his body, Mary stopped, turned to Connie and said, "Excuse me, I'm sorry, I might cry," but she stood stoic and never did.

This brutal seemingly needless act of torturous murder brought Mary's 3-year Deer relationship to a close and it was a long time before she could even talk about it. To this very day the mention of it brings a flash of pain across her face that she usually hides very well, except from the keen observer.

Sometime later, Mary did have one more surviving male Deer, which had lived separated from the dead ones and he escaped from his pen. The locals knew when they saw him, he was Mary's Deer and called in their sightings, but no one could catch him. She was relieved that he did finally wander back home on his own but he still could not be caught or penned. Logan went out with his rifle and put an end to the roaming. It just had to be done! They butchered him and put him in the freezer so as not to waste the meat.

The irony is quite apparent, for it is quite a reversal that a domestic Dog becomes wild and a wild Deer becomes domestic. Wild Dogs are a frequent problem in the Chilcotin. Many start out as pets and are neglected to the point of starvation and a high-percentage are abused so badly that they become refugees from their owners and pack-up in search of food kinship and protection from other wild animals and the elements. They attack domestic animals to survive, and have been known to attack children. This should be an expected result of the severe physical and psychological abuses man bestows on the animal he claims to be his best friend.

More Escapees on the Lamb

During the days of late October in 2006 as the ice began to form around the edges of the Bay in front of Mary's Place, bad luck was in the works. Her pet Trumpeter Swan and one of her Snow Geese managed to sneak off together and she knew she had to hurry and get them back before the ice covered the entire lake. There'd be no hope of catching them once they were able to climb up and run across the lake. She called and lured, trying to trick and catch her Swan but he kept running onto thin ice where he couldn't be followed. They'd break through into the water and swim out of reach. There was no way the Swan wanted to come in, just like a kid not wanting to come home for dinner.

After a few days doing all she could to get them into the pen she got a call from some neighbors across the lake who said they had seen three Wolves tear apart both her Swan and her Goose. She wasn't so quick to blame the Wolves, as so many do. She figured it was more likely three wild Dogs and the neighbors confused them with Wolves. Sometimes you can't tell the difference between them unless you really know your breeds. She knows all too well that more often than not, it is wild Dogs that do the killing. "Wolves get blamed for far more than their share!" she said.

She originally started out with three Swans two years earlier, but now that her last Swan had been killed, she was Swanless. She'd had Geese around for as long as she'd been at Nimpo Lake, but those too had dwindled down to one Sabastapole in mourning, honking in the direction he last saw his partner. He started wandering around with the Llamas who he seemed to have adopted as his surrogate family, kind of like Mary's Guinea Hen who frets whenever the two blue Peacocks are out of sight.

The End of a Thief

There are Mink around Mary's Place pretty much all the time but there has never been one lucky enough to get into her Chicken house, let alone steal a Chicken. But with the winter of 2007 being what it was with the higher than usual numbers of wild animals hanging around making trouble, one Mink did manage to find an opportunity to exercise his jaws and murdered at least one of Mary's birds. She dealt with him the only way a critter like that can be.

"I seen him, I went to feed my Chickens in the afternoon and there he was and I'd seen him once before, a black streak and I wasn't sure what it was. I thought it was probably a Mink but I didn't see him then. The next day I went down there and I was getting' eggs and feedin' the Chickens and there's this Mink lookin' right at me. I didn't know what got my Chicken but I found feathers and a body so I figured, well, the Mink had gotten my Chicken. The feathers were outside and the Chicken was inside with his head off. The Mink had crossed my mind. So I figured, well, I'll go get my trap because you only get one chance. A dead Chicken and I found he was eatin' eggs. Well that was it! Eggshells were all in behind the boards. I figured that's it for you, cuz they won't stop! So I went and got my trap and set it for that night. The Chicken was still out there so I cut off a leg and put it there. That was his bait. This little stinker stole my Chicken and the trap went off and I didn't catch him. So I thought, well I'll try this again. That was the next morning there. So I set the trap again. I had to be pretty cautious about it because the Chickens would have got caught in it. I thought, well, I don't know if I'll catch him or not but I'll give it a try. So I went down there a few hours later and there he was just lookin' at me, so I'd caught him. He tried to get me of course, so I moved my plywood and gently used a two-by-four. That was the end of his life. There's always Mink around but I've never had one in my barn. Never! I had a Marten one time and he killed two Ducks. There's lots of Mink around and they steal fish but I've never had one in the barn," explained Mary.

Just about the same time as the Mink was meeting his end, Mary saw a Red Fox with a limp coming up the road from her Chicken barn. "That Fox, he'd been around for an hour or so cuz this morning it snowed and I seen his tracks all over the place. But he hasn't gotten anything yet. Cuz I lock everything up, sorta. If he went down there now he could get something. I let them all out now, the Chickens, Geese, and Peacocks. But hopefully he goes on his way somewhere," she said.

Logan's Wings

Pretty much everyone around Mary's Place is a pilot and have at least one airplane and it didn't take long for Mary's partner, Logan, to fall in love with flying. He'd had enough of sitting in the passenger seat and decided he was going to take the steering into his own hands.

"Well, my first flying experience was when I lived in Sydney, and a guy had a Cessna 172 he had owned for years and years. So his family got kinda bored flying with him so he called me up and said, you wanna go for a ride? So we'd do things like run over to Chilliwack for breakfast. He'd buy the gas and I'd buy the breakfast, and we both had a good day, and it was fun flying around. It was neat to see the world from up there in a small plane. He was a good pilot and didn't do scary stuff. After I moved up here well everyone's got a floatplane. So I got lots of rides. I kind of realized later that when these guys 'er giving me rides I was just a good excuse to go for a fly! So I had lots of rides around, saw lots of neat stuff. And I soon realized that it's a waste in this country to not have a floatplane! So I started kinda perusing the airplane want ads and most of 'em were too expensive, but a few of 'em looked like they were cheap enough to afford. So I asked Harry how they would be on floats, and flying in and out of the mountains. And he said, none of 'em would do because they were too small or under-powered, or wouldn't take-off on floats. So he said the only thing that would do is a Supercub in this country. So I started lookin' at Supercubs. A decent Supercub on floats is pretty close to a hundred-grand or more, so I thought that was too expensive a toy for me and I kind of gave-up on the idea. But I kept looking at different airplanes, tryin' to get Terry's input on what might work and what I could get for cheaper. So I was looking around trying to see what I could buy and upgrade, and see how I could make something work. Some of them would've worked but they would have been barely good enough and we wouldn't have been able to get in and out of Wilderness Lake (Mary's remote cabin). And that was about twenty percent of the reason we wanted an airplane. Then... Brian from Wilderness Rim Resort down the lake decided he wanted to sell his Supercub. He bought it from a Northwest Territory rancher as an investment. It was kind of ratty, and he was gonna fix it up and make some money on it and then they decided to move their operation (Pioneer Log Homes) to Williams Lake. So he was kind-of thinning out his inventory of stuff and he figured he could do just fine with his Beaver and his 185. So he said he'd sell me the Supercub for what he had in it. Well I wanted it, but I didn't think it was a good time to get it. So I was waffling back and forth because we're building a new house.

Then one day Mary saw me looking at a floatplane flying over the lake. She saw me gazing at it. She said, "Oh, the house can wait, go buy your airplane!" So I thought about that for about a nanosecond and we called and made the deal. All of a sudden I owned a Supercub on floats! There was no sleep that night! And then the next reality hit me. I didn't have a license to fly an airplane! So as luck would have it one of our neighbors is a flight instructor and he said he would teach me how to do it, so that was cool. But it took so long because he was gone a lot and didn't have much time. So I bought the airplane in May. Finally in October I found another guy who would teach me. So now I'm flyin' on my own! There's such a big difference between riding in an airplane with somebody and flyin' one yourself, cuz you can go where you wanna, go zoom around, do turns and stalls and fly around the mountains. You can go and look at what you want to look at instead of lookin' at what's going by when someone else is doin' the flying. Plus, being in control of the thing. It's not really dangerous it's just that it's your ass up there. You're responsible for yourself and that makes it a little bit more exciting. The first time I took the controls actually was in Terry's airplane. We were flyin' on skis in the wintertime quite a bit. I was always askin' him questions about what he was doing and what-if this and what-if that, all kinds of questions. And then one day I went out there and I was fixin' to climb in the backseat of his Supercub, and Terry said you get in the front today! And I couldn't believe he said that! My disbelief kinda made him smile. Well he said, you can do this! So he told me what to do and what to expect. He said when I get to forty miles an hour the thing will just fly. We got to forty miles and hour and we were flyin'. My heart was way above where the airplane was but it was just fantastic! We flew around for about an hour over to Charlotte Lake, and we went in over Anahim Lake and just kinda flew around a bit. But then we came home and when we got close to the lake I fully expected him to take over from the backseat because I know from flying radio controlled airplanes that's the dangerous part. But he just told me what to do and what to expect and kept an eye on me, and I landed it! I was hooked then! I was so excited I was kind-of shakin'. And when I came down I thought I gotta have me one of these!" said Logan.

So after a calm glassy day he was a flyer, and after enough takeoffs and landings the umbilical was cut and he was on his own and happy to lose the extra weight of an instructor he'd towed around in the backseat throughout the learning curve. Now you can look up in the sky on many a perfect day and see him in his little blue and white Supercub, doing flybys over the house. Not long after he bought his plane he stripped the fabric off and recovered the whole thing, except the wings which he decided to do later. Even and expert said he did a pretty darn good job.

Green Weasel & the Fisher

During December of 2006, a weird critter showed up at Mary's Place. It was a bizarre luminescent green Weasel. I'd seen him lurking around the property at the bird feeders leaping through the deep powder snow. Everyone, including Mary looked at me with a more than slightly raised eyebrow, thinkin' I was crazy for claiming to have seen a critter that glowed green. But I knew he was real because I'd been trying to keep him from getting into my cabin. He'd shown a keen interest in coming through the door, sometimes standing on a woodpile outside the window peering in at me. So as I walked out the door to take a handful of peanuts to the birds and decided to try and trap him I immediately saw a Mink, another member of the Weasel family, exiting the doghouse near the bird area. He was a beautiful chocolate black/brown with a fluffy tail and a body much like a Weasel and not much bigger. I took chase after him because I knew he wouldn't hesitate to eat my birds or my little canine if he got a chance. He bounded over the snow and through some seed I had scattered on the ground. He seemed to be gone, and after a few minutes a River Otter from a nearby den showed up about fifteen feet away, behind a snow bank. I watched him as he wandered off then I moved to the right of a hanging feeder station where I had been standing and was thinking to myself that maybe one of my birds was hiding in a snow-covered willow-hollow nearby. So I pushed the branches to the side and bent down to look inside the hollow. The birds often hide food in there (a dangerous thing to do in this country).

I was feeling very casual and relaxed with my handful of peanuts but still had the green Weasel in the back of my mind. I bent further down toward the snow-covered ground to see inside the dark hollow and I was sort of in a state of relaxed disconnect, not really thinking about much at all except that darn Weasel. Then I thought I saw some dark eyes in the hollow and wondered if it was the Mink again. So I bent even further down and leaned toward the entrance. My face ended up only about two feet away from the entrance, very low to the ground. By this time I was squatting down on my haunches peering in, searching for the dark eyes I thought I'd seen, and there were the eyes again, looking out from a dark face.

At first I thought Raccoon, then I thought maybe a Badger (another member of the Weasel family), but I had never actually seen a Badger except in cartoons so I had no real-life image to compare this critter to. I moved in for an even closer look and his were fixed on me, unflinching. Our eyes were locked, totally focused and oddly we sat like that for about ten seconds until I said, "Well, who the hell are you?" I was still feeling very casual though, and for some reason I wasn't alarmed. I saw no birds around that could be in any danger. The moment just didn't register as threatening because most animals here run from humans, and I must have decided in the back of my brain that as soon as I was finished observing this animal, I'd send him running like I had the Mink and Otter.

We continued to stare at each other with me down at his level, bent right over with my face in his face, I of course, in the vulnerable position. I leaned forward a bit and he could have ripped my face off at any time. After I decided he wasn't going to move I suddenly noticed that he had a golden orange brow. I ruled out Otter, Muskrat, Weasel, and Mink. Hmmm, I wondered stupidly. Then I sort of backed away and raised myself back up to a standing position. As I did, I said out loud. "Ok, get out of here now! Go on, get out". And I began clapping my hands together. Then I just turned and walked back to my cabin, but on my way in I thought, hey I'll grab my camera and snap a photo. So I went back out to the hollow with my camera but he was gone. With all that snow everywhere if he were hiding in some other sneaky spot watching me, I wouldn't have known.

I never saw hide or hair of him the rest of that day and I asked Mary if it could possibly have been a Badger or Raccoon. "Nope not around here, none of those around!" she said shaking her head adamantly. So I scratched my head a little bit over my puzzling encounter and recalled Mary and Logan said they'd seen a Wolverine across the lake on the ice a few days earlier so I wondered if this could be that animal. I had never actually seen one, only a side-view in some of the photos Logan had taken. He got some good Wolverine shots the winter before while out riding his snow machine on the frozen lake.

I went and searched for photos of Badgers on the Internet. The ones I saw looked nothing like the coloring I had seen. The animal I had encountered was very dark with an orange brow. I typed "Fisher" into the Google Search Engine, not thinking for one second that it would end up being the spitting image of the animal I had seen, but it was, brother to the Wolverine. I was shocked. The Fisher returned for regular visits and often his tracks in the snow couldn't be deciphered from a Wolverine, except they were a bit smaller. Both have a very similar track and gait.

Mary was out tracking that animal almost daily. One day she was out looking and brought home a bit of scat and rolled it around in her fingers to show me all the birdseed that was in it. "You're attracting him with all that bird seed!" she said. Often, the Fisher would sit on the old Doghouse eating food I'd put out for the camp robbers. You couldn't tell him to leave or scare him off and he'd sit and eat every morsel of whatever food was there till it was gone, bread, spagetti, birdseed. He'd look you right in the eye while he did it too, often showing his white fangs that reminded me of a Vampire or Cat, which might be why some call Fishers, Fisher-Cats. You wouldn't want to mess with that critter on your healthiest day, I figure.

So, then comes the green Weasel again. At first nobody believed that he was real until Logan and Connie saw him at the Chicken barn. I think everyone was questioning their own sanity for a while, wondering if maybe they'd been victims of the power of suggestion. On December 01/2006, I was out visiting my Chickadee feeder and there were several feet of white powder on the ground. Something started flicking, digging, and shoveling around under the snow. Then a tiny white head popped up pushing the snow away. He looked this way and that way, then popped the rest of his body out. My birds curiously tilted their heads to one side as they watched this critter in the snowdrift. Then he bounded along in short, quick pouncing spurts. It was a little white Weasel with a black tipped tail; only he wasn't exactly white. Well, he was white but I noticed right away that he had a distinct luminescent green hue to his fur, the color of antifreeze and I was stunned.

First I tried to tell myself it was some reflection off the snow, but it wasn't. I blinked hard to try and clear my eyes to get a better look. This little guy clearly had glowing green fur. Even the snow took-on a green glow as he moved along. If he had inadvertently been doused in antifreeze he would be dead or at least very ill but he was as healthy as any animal I'd ever seen.

I followed him with my camera as he jerked around, seemingly confused, as if not to know where he was, or which direction he wanted to travel in, just flitting around. I really had to concentrate on focusing my camera and was lucky enough to get a few good shots. I must have spooked him and he tunneled into another snowdrift beside my log cabin and disappeared.

Weasels love to eat birds so he was obviously at my chickadee feeder for a reason, not just to show off. Although Weasels aren't much bigger than your typical squirrel, pound per pound they are said to be the most vicious animal of all the fur bearers, able to kill animals several times their size. They will often enter an animal's den and kill it by wrapping its body around the victim's throat and chewing the base of the brain stem. They eat the brain and drink the blood, whichever they're in the mood for, or simply leave the animal there to rot and proceed to hunt and kill many more animals, haul them into the den and let the bodies pile up, eating only one or two. They are one of the few animals that indulge in overkill for seemingly no reason.

Eventually I did trap that little bugger. One night at dusk I had just closed up the cabin for the night. I was settling in on the couch for a little relaxation when I heard the unmistakable snap of my rat-trap on the porch. I swung open the door and squeamishly looked to see what was in there. It was the Weasel, and he was as dead as a nail.

I ran up to Mary's Place and was clean out of breath by the time I arrived. "I got him, I got him, the green Weasel, in my trap," I said.

Now I could prove the green Weasel's existence once and for all. Logan swung down and picked him up from the trap because I didn't want to touch him. We took him up to Mary's and everyone crowded around and took a good look. Finally Mary believed me. But it was his skin that was glowing the green, which caused his fur to glow against the snow whenever he bounded around. The color appeared to be completely unnatural.

Logan's mother Doris and Mary both had a-go at rolling him around in their hands for a close examination and picked through his fur as the lice jumped off. There was a lot of head scratching going on over what made him glow green. There he was, larger than life, or should I say dead on the counter. No one could say he didn't glow.

Of course, a call went out to the government to see if they'd like to have the Weasel for lab tests but nobody called back. Mary hung him in a plastic bag outside her door for a week or two where he remained frozen with his face pushed up against the inside of the bag, with the outline of the mouth and eyes showing through. There he hung as a conversation piece until we could decide what to do with him.

Mary called a fur trapper and asked him if he'd have any use for a green Weasel and wasn't much interested. Finally she got sick of looking at him hanging by her door and tossed him into her wood stove.

A friend of Mary's suggested that liver disease could cause a glowing green hue to the skin. Her idea on the cause of the green color went into the mixing bowl of possibilities, which ranged from the Weasel having been an escaped lab animal, to having been contaminated with Uranium. The mystery lives on.

Moose Calf Kill

Sometime in January 2007 Mary saw a sight she loves to see. Three Moose standing not too far from her living room window on the frozen snow-covered lake-ice. There was a Bull, a Cow, and a Calf all together. As she stood gazing, she said, "It's a beautiful sight to see. At least we know there are Moose around!" She was pleased to see a Moose several weeks earlier on the road leading into her place not too far beyond the cattle-guard, just rolling and digging around in the deep snow trying to expose the grasses beneath. He didn't seem alarmed at all when people passed by.

There were Coyotes all around too, calling and yapping back and forth to each other during the nights and early mornings, sometimes even during the afternoons. There were tracks all over the place. Then one morning she saw a Coyote carrying what looked like a stick of wood on the lake-ice. She realized right away that this was no stick and jumped on her snow-machine and rode out to the nearby Bay to see what had been killed. As she drove out there, she wasn't quite sure what she'd find but knew she would find some sort of carcass! Even from a distance it was easy to see the remains. A pack of Wolves or possibly even a Wolverine had killed and devoured a Moose Calf. She had seen a Wolverine on the lake-ice a month or so earlier so there was definitely one in the vicinity and it could have been the culprit.

The Calf's gut-pile was intact and there was a remnant of one hind-leg and fur strewn everywhere. The shredded carcass bits covered an area of maybe thirty-feet or so and there were bird tracks all around the remains. Some Eagle, Coyote, and Wolf tracks seemed evident. No doubt the Fisher had checked things out as well... as it seemed every other animal in the woods had.

She wasn't sure if the dead Calf was the one she saw earlier with the Bull and the Cow on the lake or not. There were plenty of Moose around that year. It seemed to be that every time you'd turn around someone saw a Moose and that made Mary happy because she's always been worried about the Moose population around these parts, that they'd been over-hunted. It appeared at least this year the Moose were flourishing.

She found some scant remains of a Deer at a bay a bit further down the lake a few days later. It looked like there was lots of prey and certainly plenty of predators to balance things out, a regular smorgasboard. Never in all her forty years had she seen so many wild animals around, and the presence of Wolves on the lake-ice seemed to astonish her. She's seen wild Dogs, Coyotes, and the like, but never have the Wolves come in so close before. She attributed the high number of animals hanging around to the deep snow and nature's cycles of abundance and scarcity.

The winter of 2007 was a wild one in terms of weather, lots of wind and more snow than you could plow. Even after a bit of melting, three feet of snow stubbornly stuck making it difficult for Moose to get around and more vulnerable to predators. So the Wolves made hay while the hayin' was good. "Wildlife is not for eating! That's what farm animals are for! There are not enough animals left in the wild to be hunting them!" she said.

Itcha Crash

August 8th 2006 was a blustery day and Mary was outside burning tree branches and pinecones. By about 3:00 PM she had a good fire on the go and she radiated a rosy glow from the wind and the heat of the flames sweeping across her face. She was trying to keep busy while she awaited news about one of Stewart's Lodge's planes that was late returning after an afternoon excursion over the Itcha Mountains. She thought it was a perfectly beautiful day for working outside, even in the rain, which had interrupted the sun and given her a good dousing for a couple of hours. She busied herself raking pinecones into piles and forking them into the fire as her friend Floyd, a seasoned pilot flew around to see if he could spot the tardy airplane.

A couple of hours later she and Logan were sitting down to dinner with a few close friends, Frank and Claudia, and Henry and Florence, when a transmission came over the aviation radio next to the table. It was Floyd conversing with his wife Laura while she was making a contact with Tweedsmuir Air, trying to get a bearing on each other's locations. Floyd bore the news that he'd seen the wreckage and Search and Rescue were just about to land at the scene of the crash. The plane had been shattered and both the pilot and passenger had been killed. This was the first ever accident for Stewart's Lodge and a sad day for a lot of folks.

Planes often go down in these rugged mountains because bush-flying is inherently dangerous and when most of your friends are pilots you live with the reality that any one of them could be suddenly taken from your life. Although Mary did not know this new summer pilot personally, she was saddened. It can happen to the best, and often does. Her heart was with the families of the lost souls and her friends who owned the plane.

Funeral in the Woods

Barely a night had passed since Mary cooked to feed one hundred and twenty hungry people at the February 17th 2007, 139-club-telethon fundraiser dinner/auction, when she was busy again. February 18th, she set out looking for a gravesite for Karl Grundmann, a long-time friend who had just passed away. Born on November 19th, 1921... he died on February 13th 2007 just two days after Mary's birthday. On February 19th a backhoe set to digging through two feet of snow into the frozen rocky volcanic soil, until finally a hole was properly dug.

Four surviving members of Karl's family, Peter, Warner, Ingrid, and Sarah, arrived at Mary's Place accompanying Karl's coffin. They had a permit to escort his body in a white tinted-windowed van which stayed parked overnight on the gravel in the driveway in front of Mary's doorstep while inside the house Karl's family was warmly greeted and fed.

She had been cooking during the early part of the day in anticipation of their arrival. That's just the way she takes care of people. She quietly and respectfully met their need for comfort by addressing their tummies, lending them a shoulder, and an ear, not to mention a roof, a bed, and a shower.

Karl and his wife Irma had visited Mary's resort for as long as she owned the land, thirty-eight years. Prior to moving to Nanoose Bay on Vancouver Island, Karl owned a blueberry farm in Richmond. But no matter where he lived year-round, he traveled to Nimpo Lake every summer to visit Mary's Place and he and Irma thought of her the same way many people do, as kin. If it weren't for the rest of Karl's family not taking as much of an interest in the place as he did, he'd have moved to Nimpo years ago.

Mary's Chilcotin was where Karl and Irma's hearts lived, so when the end came for each of them, it was the place they chose to be buried. First went Karl's mother Gertrud who had not visited much. Then his wife Irma passed and Karl laid both to rest in the Chilcotin. Now Karl himself was gone and it had come to past that the long picturesque drive they had all taken so many times together as a family in life, had finally been taken separately in death. This, Karl's final five hundred mile trip to Nimpo would see him back again with those who went before him. This last-of-three Chilcotin-bound souls lay in repose on this, his final night on Earth.

Inside Mary's Place, the wood stove burned warmly and the lights from inside the house cast an amber glow out the window into the darkness onto the crisp wilderness snow. It brings a strange feeling to think about a man being gone. A man who's eye had scanned the horizon gazing at sunrises and sunsets. A man who's feet had navigated the landscape under a vast expanse of sky ...a sky that received his voice as it echoed off the mountains right after he snagged a good catch on his fly rod. You might easily sense the presence of a man whose heart is one with this wilderness on a quiet evening, or during the early mornings when the call of the Coyotes break the stillness.

The next morning with the temperature hovering around minus eleven degrees, Mary came out of the Chicken barn with a few eggs she gathered before leaving for the funeral. She tried not to appear solemn but her face was rife with emotion. She had a good cry the day before. As tough as she is, she's really just as soft as the cookie dough she makes. Friendships are her pride and joy, and it broke her heart to see the end of Karl's visits, his chatter, and the end of an era. She would have to find something else to fill the spaces that he and Irma had filled over the years.

Karl had lived a good long life, but now he would be laid to rest in the presence of Karl's brother Warner, his wife Ingrid, his son Peter, and his grand daughter Sarah, and Mary, Logan, and Connie stood close by. They all shared lunch afterwards and then the farewells were spoken and Karl's family headed out onto the highway toward home again. They would return during the summer to bring Karl's headstone.

With Karl on her mind, Mary set about doing the rest of her daily chores. She now had two Roosters on her mind, which had to go because they were hybrids and were too much trouble in the Chicken house. She would butcher them within a couple of days and put them in the freezer...but not today. Karl's death had caused her to reflect on her own life. When you're saying final good-byes to folks you've known half your life, friends who loved you enough that they came to your home every year for a good portion of their own lives, they have to be taking a bit of you with them when they go. "I feel privileged that they always came here. Karl probably would not have come all these years if it wasn't for my family!" said Mary.

Early next morning found her in the Chicken barn butchering the two Roosters, which she then placed in boiling water to loosen the follicles, then she removed the feathers. They were quickly cleaned and put onto plates on the kitchen counter, until she could decide whether to freeze or roast them.

By late morning she was baking cookies for some folks she and Logan had met at the BC Floatplane Association meeting last summer. She had received a last minute call from some pilots who wanted to give her a sudden visit. The first plane on skis buzzed Mary's roof just after noontime and promptly landed on the lake-ice and taxied to the dock. The other two planes followed in shortly after. Just more new friends dropping in from Williams Lake for an afternoon visit.

On August 22nd 2007, the Grundmann family traveled back to Mary's Place with Karl's headstone. She went out to the Anahim cemetery, which had only about a half dozen occupied plots. There was no road going in off the main road... so she drove in over the large boulders strewn along the makeshift path. Blue Dragonflies fluttered past in double-decker mating style over the plaques and through the trees signaling the cycle of life as she tidied up the graves, pulled weeds, and repositioned the silk flowers that had blown around over the winter. She made sure everything looked respectable and then closed the gate and tied a loose knot in the rope behind her as she left, so that the Grundmanns' wouldn't have to struggle with it.

They came, they fished, and they installed Karl's headstone and gave Mary a stainless steel bird feeder with decorated stained glass walls and a halogen light inside, a virtual birdie retreat. They stayed for three days, then headed back home.

Wicked Wildfires of 2004 & 2006

Mary described her involvement in helping the authorities during the 2004 wildfire that ravaged the Atnarko River and Lonesome Lake area near Bella Coola, the latter which obliterated the historic Edwards homestead in Tweedsmuir park.

"As soon as you see smoke in this country you wonder where it's comin' from! The wind brought the smoke this way. The fire never got close to us in any way, shape or form. The Charlotte Lake people were on evacuation notice. But that's a laugh because we all know now. I had helicopter pilots come in here. They had their fire center at the airport like they always do and they were feeding 400 fire fighters. And it was typical camp stuff. Well, the pilots, they always think they're a little bit further up the ladder and they don't want to eat that camp stuff so they came over here and occupied three or four cabins, and stayed here! There were seven of 'em I would guess, because I had to keep track of everything. I doubt it was ten days I don't think it was two weeks they were here. I don't even remember where I put 'em all! They rotated. There wasn't always seven here. There might have been three or four. They'd have a few days off and they rotated around or they'd go home or whatever they did. All in all, I went through seven different pilots. Two or three times they stopped over here, over at Terry's but they had to leave their helicopters at the airport. The base was there and the fuel was there, and everything was there. I had a helicopter land right here a couple times but the fire ones landed over on the cement. I fed 'em all the meals there was to feed 'em. I think I packed lunches for them. Depending on what they were doin'. They only work so many hours and then they've gotta have a break, so it just depended on what their days consisted of. You know they'd start at 9:30 in the morning. They never went before 9:30. Some of 'em went by 10:00. It always varied. The fire never came anywhere near here. You use common sense, the fire was way over there. It wasn't getting' way over here. There's no way it was! The Edwards place went up in the early part of the fire. That was the big issue, they wouldn't put any fire fighters in there. So it became a big monumental issue. Cuz they let it burn! They wouldn't have fire fighters in there because it was in the park. See, you're not supposed to be fightin' fire in the park. They were down there with helicopters all the time. But they couldn't fight the fire because they have to do what they're told to. They went to get John Edwards out. He did go eventually. I remember two or three stories between that and the TV and whatever. They looked after him very well once they realized they were all in the wrong. The government looked after him really well. I know they took him back and forth for things, to take stuff out. He was always worrying about his Foxy. He got all the stuff he wanted out. His Foxes just went someplace else. They never burnt up or anything because when he went back afterwards, there was Foxy waitin' for him. That was all over the news about his Fox Vicky. He had all kinds of them, more than one Fox. The one, Vicky, was his pet," explained Mary.

During the summer of 2006, another fire ravaged somewhere in the neighborhood of twelve thousand hectares of Chilcotin wilderness around the Dean River area. The authorities went to Mary and served her a two-hour evacuation alert and asked if she wanted to be put on the evacuation list, or if she intended to stay in the event that the fire got too close. She opted to stay behind, so they put a line of tape across the dirt road just on the other side of the cattle-guard, to let rescuers know that Mary's Place was to be left alone. There was plenty of fire fighting equipment, water pumps, hoses, and heavy equipment on hand, to build a fireguard if it became necessary. There were also a few experienced pilots with planes who lived nearby. Between all of them, they decided they could handle any emergency themselves.

As the media continually reported that Anahim and Nimpo Lake had been evacuated, everyone went about their day to day activities. No one really had been evacuated. They made a lot to do about nothing. Someone flew up over the fire and took a peek to see how big it was, and saw that the darn thing was nearly extinguished, with only a few spot fires smoldering. The media didn't report that. The whole world thought the place was up in flame and people were in a panic, but that wasn't true. Unfortunately the annual Rodeo was cancelled as a result of the bologne, which hurt the local merchants that rely on it to make a living. The entire incident was so overblown by the media. It couldn't have been good for tourism. If you flipped on the TV and saw on the news that your summer vacation destination was ablaze and on evacuation notice, would you cancel?

That summer turned-out heavy losses for the Chilcotin, particularly around Nimpo and Anahim. The Mountain Pine Beetle ravaged the plateau. It was suggested that an area the size of Sweden had effected British Columbia, which apparently turned out to be a bonus for mining interests. Stewart's Lodge suffered their first-ever plane crash, resulting in the loss of two lives in the Itcha Mountains. The local sawmill shut down and some families packed-up and left in search of work. There were rumors that it might re-open after some political matters were settled but some families didn't have time for that to be sorted out. Hungry stomachs come first. Eventually the mill was up and running again, and some folks returned but not everyone.

The Nimpo Motel burned to the ground and the Chilcotin Gate restaurant closed its doors. That had been Mary's restaurant years earlier and it was called Mary's Place back then. It burnt down back in 1996, but she rebuilt it in '97. The builders had to light fires to keep the cement from freezing, so they could pour it. So she was deeply saddened to see it sold because she wondered what the Charlotte Lake folks would do when they came to town. There'd be no place for them to take a rest, have any refreshments, or get a bite to eat. That bothered her!

A lot of fishing lodges went on the market, and some went bankrupt due to the downward trend. Many Americans cancelled their fishing trips due to fears of being caught in wildfires or maybe contracting West Nile virus. There was also the ever-looming threat of terrorism. Whether that threat is real, imagined, or conjured, is debatable, however there are plenty of border delays as a consequence. But some regulars just didn't want to see what the Pine Beetle had done to their beloved wilderness vacation spots. The forests on the plateau began recovering very quickly though, with Poplar and Spruce shooting up like weeds everywhere to fill in the gaps. Still, it was a sad sight to see so many dead Pine trees. Even though West Nile had yet to rear it's head in British Columbia, there can be no way to forget the embattlement a person faces here during the summer months in the Chilcotin. Swarming Mosquitoes are simply part of your day, and I mean big ones, so big that when you swat 'em they go clunk when they drop on the table. Not that these things ever effected Mary's business. Her resort is one of the few that continues to stay solidly booked.

Chance Meeting on the Stairs
with John Edwards

One of Mary's important friendships was the one she had with a well-known eighty-one year-old wilderness recluse John Edwards (now deceased). Here we had a true bushman who came from a long line of bushmen who homesteaded at Lonesome Lake in the heart of Tweedsmuir park near Bella Coola. John made friends with the wild animals of his landscape surrounding himself with Foxes, Martens and other critters. He survived Cougar and Grizzly Bear attacks and experienced the kind of life few men ever imagine, let alone recall.

He spent most of his life on the property settled by his father, Ralph Edwards in 1912. His family became world famous after Pulitzer Prize winning author, Leland Stowe wrote a book in 1957 about the Edwards all-out efforts to save a dwindling flock of Trumpeter Swans, titled, 'Crusoe of Lonesome Lake'. There have been several books written about his family over the years, and his sister Trudy has a few of her own in print.

In 2004 a wildfire savagely whipped across the Atnarko Valley destroying John's family land, his home, and two generations of personal belongings. Barely outrunning the fire he made his escape on foot carrying little more than a backpack and his manuscripts. There was no time to remove much of anything else or to save his Foxes, which had to be left to fend for themselves. He was afraid they wouldn't outrun the fire and that he'd never see them again. But when he returned to his homestead after the fire destroyed the cabin, his Foxes came looking for him and he couldn't believe it. He thought they were dead for sure and even if they had survived there was nothing left to come back to, nothing recognizable! The fire raged to the level of a class-six, the worst measurement you could have.

John came out of what was left of his remote wilderness homestead, three or four times a year to get supplies or do whatever business needed to be done. Then he went back in with the Grizzlies. There are no access roads in to his place so he drove his old truck as far as he could and walked the remaining two-hour stretch in, passing many a Grizzly along his route. His brother Stanley had gone missing some years before and they were unable to locate him for months. He had died in the outhouse and no one thought to look there. Though John's regular communications with the outside world happened much later and was unrelated to his brother's death, it was probably some comfort to folks that the arrangements had been made to stay in touch. Maybe a similar circumstance could be avoided. His calls to Mary from his place at Lonesome Lake twice a week let everyone know he was ok. The deal was, if Mary didn't hear from him, the posse would go out.

I was lucky enough to meet John on February 13 2007 at about 3:30 in the afternoon during one of his occasional trips out to civilization. He was just leaving Mary's when I was there to pick up my ration of eggs. She came to the door and when I told her I had come for eggs she whispered that John was there and just leaving. She, John, and Logan were just getting up off the couch after what had obviously been a good long chat and Logan was suggesting that he had a long drive ahead and maybe should think about getting going. I heard Logan ask John, "So what are the top three things you've survived? Cougar attacks, Bear attacks, so what's the third one?" There was a pause before Logan put a few words in his mouth, "Being born?" They both laughed and moved out of the living room into the hallway. I don't know if that was a private joke that implied John had come into the world in as an exciting fashion as he lived, but I think so. I wished I'd been a fly on the wall during that conversation. Logan was seeing him to the door and as they came toward the stairs I was just inside the door and came face to face with the wild man everyone always talked about. His name often came up at the cash register in stores, around dinner tables, and in the media. My timing couldn't have been better, I thought. Just to be able to meet him was a peak-life-experience!

Mary introduced us and we began to talk right away. She said, "You don't need me here for this," and handed me a dozen eggs, squeezed between us, and headed out to the Chicken barn. Contrary to some descriptions of him, that he was a weird old man with a knotted-beard, I found him to be well-groomed, polite, and a most exciting and animated conversationalist who immediately offered up stories about his adventures in the wilderness, stories you never forget. We spent about twenty minutes or so on the steps and he readily answered my questions and spoke about his life, family, homestead, and about the fire that wiped it out. He talked about his Foxes, the wild animal attacks he'd survived as if he instinctively knew I wanted to hear about it, and I did. He crammed a lot into twenty minutes. I listened carefully as he described several adventures, and spoke of government conspiracies surrounding his family homestead, and about how he felt his lawyer betrayed him to the government instead of working for him. He said he was writing about his wilderness life and his relationship with the animals, his Squirrels, Martens, and particularly his Foxes that he considered family. He said he was documenting the years with his wild friends for the world to read. He told me about how he sued the BC government for failing to protect his ancestor's 1912 cabin and outbuildings from the Atnarko fire. He said the government didn't want old homesteaders on parkland anymore and that he was upset that they let the flames rip through, all the while taking steps to protect other properties in the valley and that he was determined to rebuild his homestead. He said he won his case in court and a substantial settlement and upon researching the news archives, I found what he said to be true. He said he was coming back on July 7th to speak at the BC Floatplane Association meeting. I told him I wanted to build my own log cabin with my own hands someday and he extended an offer for me to contact him anytime with questions about log cabin building. He told me that his manuscript might be ready in a year or so... and it would be titled "A Tale of Two Foxes." A tall slender man with startling blue eyes, he stood on the second to the top step towering over me as I stood at the bottom beside the door.

I told him I would love to hear all his stories. He piped up and said "July 7th, I'll be here then. You hear me? July 7th! I'll be back and we can talk on July 7th!" he repeated. "I will definitely be around for that!" I replied anxiously. Then he told me about how one time when he was out hunting, and walking back to his cabin carrying Deer meat, he suddenly sensed that he wasn't alone. He had his rifle in his hands and Deer meat on his back. While standing there at the top of the stairs, he spun around to show me how he turned and planted the firing end of his rifle on a lunging Cougar's chest, which made me nervous that he might slip and fall, after-all, he was over eighty years old. The fire in his eyes made it seem that he was right back there in that moment. What a storyteller he was! He said the Cougar had crept up behind him and lunged at his back. "The end of my gun came to rest right on his chest as I turned around without a second to spare. The distance between me and his chest was exactly the length of my gun with no room to spare!" he said vividly as he spread his hands apart to indicate the distance. "I shot him dead instantly! So the Deer won that time!" he laughed. "You get it?" he repeated as he smiled and looked me right in the eye. "The Deer won? I was wearing this very coat that I'm wearing right now!" he explained. He continued to laugh heartily as he smoothed his hand over his sleeve to show me the coat's perfect condition. I laughed along with him only half-hearted because I wasn't sure that it was a laughing matter. If it had been me in that situation I don't know that I'd have been able to look back on it so casually or fondly.

He went from one story to the next and talked about another time he'd been to town for supplies and on his way back he drove his truck as far as he could along the dirt road and parked it at the usual place. He began his two-hour hike the rest of the way in to his homestead at Lonesome Lake. It was normal to see Grizzly Bears on his trips in and out and they never bothered him much. But this time, as he was walking along he sensed something following fairly close behind, so he turned around and immediately felt the swiping blow of a massive paw strike him across the face. It was a Grizzly Bear that had been sauntering along behind him and John took him by surprise when he turned around. He emphasized that the Bear hadn't meant any harm and nothing would have happened if he hadn't looked back. He'd spooked him is all, and he just instinctively swiped as a result of his surprise. If he had meant to harm John, he would have eaten him right then and there, but the one swipe was the end of it. He was sporting a nasty scar down his nose though! What would scare the boots off anyone just rolled right off him.

He said he was compiling stacks of stories about his Foxes and would publish his own book and emphasized he would publish it himself, which made me think he didn't trust anyone else to do it justice. Still standing at the bottom of the steps with a dozen of Mary's eggs in my hand I paid close attention as he continued offering exciting tidbits about his fantastic life.

He'd planned to head out on the highway a bit sooner and it must have been getting close to 4:00 PM, but our incidental meeting got in the way. I could see that Logan, who was standing behind him at the top of the stairs, was aware that he'd forgotten the time so he was trying to gently nudge him on his way. He had four hours of driving ahead of him and it was getting late. My hand on the doorknob, I made like I was leaving so he could get going, but every time I turned the knob a bit John would offer another wild detail and I would relax my hand again. Even though I felt the pressure that I should just walk out the door and let him go, I was glued to his words. He seemed as happy to stand there and talk as I was to listen so I wasn't going anywhere until a real strong signal was sent for me to move along. Finally Logan moved just a little bit closer in behind him and injected a little you-better-get-going energy into the moment, which reminded us that it really was time to go. So I regretfully bit the bullet and turned the doorknob all the way over and opened the door. He started down the stairs and Logan followed slowly behind. I walked outside onto the driveway and John followed to make his way to his old red truck, which he began describing as belonging to his sister, Trudy. As I walked one way and he walked the other...he said, "This is my sister's truck. My own wouldn't have made it this far," he laughed as the distance grew between his voice and my ears.

I walked back to my cabin and marked July 7th 2007 on my calendar, crossed my fingers that nothing would go wrong, and began counting the days until I would meet John Edwards again, only for a much longer chat about his adventures.

As the winter wore on and snow continued to pile up I would occasionally ask Mary if she'd heard any more from him. She reminded me that she speaks to him on a weekly basis by satellite phone when he checks in to let her know all is well at Lonesome Lake. I mentioned to Mary that I really wanted to snap a photo of her and John together at his next visit. She couldn't understand why! I reminded her that he is a very important and historic person in the Chilcotin wilderness and that she, a historic person herself as well as a good friend of John's more than warranted a photo of the two of them together. She said she didn't think he was all that close to anyone. I had to tell her that she is as close as anyone can be to a man who lives that remotely. She, being the modest woman that she is, only reluctantly nodded in agreement. In my opinion, that's really saying something!

John was not only coming to talk with me in July 7th, but he was coming firstly to speak at the annual BC Floatplane Association meeting because Logan had talked him into doing it during his February visit. It would also be another special occasion, John's birthday, and he would be 82 years old that day. Mary would throw him a little get-together, bake a cake, and he'd speak at the meeting, and give me a little talk! What a spectacular weekend it was going to be. So many people were anxious to hear him talk about how he built his own airplane in the bush, and about his family homestead and critters, among other things.

The months dragged by and I waited for confirmation that John was still coming. Finally, with only a month or so left before the Floatplane Association meeting, she got a call from John with the news that the esophageal cancer he had surgery for the previous year had returned and he was leaving his Foxes for a while to go for chemotherapy. Mary's heart sank and mine dropped down a few stairs too! But she said John was still planning to make it for the meeting and his birthday on July 7th. I wondered if he really would be able to. Mary, being the eternal optimist she is, left the negative thoughts out of the equation. He said he was coming, and for Mary, he was coming, unless he called and said he wasn't. If, when, or until that time comes, think positive! She refused to think any other way!

After his chemotherapy he returned to his Foxes for a short while but didn't recover and had to come out of the bush to stay with his sister Trudy in Bella Coola in late June. Mary spoke to him once again and he was still determined to make it for the meeting, but it was looking more and more like someone would have to drive him because he was no longer strong enough to drive himself and was on all kinds of medication for pain. The weeks turned to days and the days dwindled to three, but still John said he was coming to the meeting. I cued up my tape recorder and made sure all the batteries were fully charged and checked my camera to make sure it was ready.

Thursday July 5th, John said he was still coming. On her way into Anahim store that day, Mary heard the song 'The Old Rugged Cross' on her truck stereo and it brought her close to tears. Someone had taped that song for her years ago right before he died, but she wouldn't say who. It was the last thing she remembers of whoever it was and she says she can barely hear it without falling apart. She was unusually melancholy, possibly she knew that John would not be coming to visit!

Friday July 6th, she spoke to John again and he told her that he would not be able to make it, and she knew what that meant. No matter how you sliced it, John was now on his deathbed. There went my interview, into the black abyss.

The first thing that came to my mind was what would his Foxes do without him? After the fire he came back and they came back, but this time, the Foxes would be on an endless quest to find him but never would again. They would have to go back into the wild from which they came and John would be their ghost for always.

Mary went about her work as the floatplanes taxied to the dock, one after the other, after the other, after the other. Some flew in on wheels and came down on the landing strip right behind her house. The Canadian military showed up for the meeting in a yellow Cormorant helicopter. She put the arriving members of the Floatplane Association into cabins, found tenting spots, and squeezed them in every which place she could find room. All-in-all she was expecting about 40 planes to show up for the weekend.

On Saturday they'd fill in the slot where John was supposed to give his talk with some last minute filler, and at night a four-piece band would put on a dance in Terry's hangar and they'd do a fly-out poker-run on Sunday. Logan flew his plane out to set up check-in-stations at five different lakes, Charlotte, Kappan, Turner, Moose, and then back to Nimpo Lake. Pilots would have to fly out to the five lakes, five parks, and land on each one to get a card and the best poker-hand would win.

It was to be a splendid few days and the weather was grand, but the gloomy shadow of John's condition and his not being able to make it for his birthday cast a real sadness around the place! Mary put on a happy face but there was little doubt that her heart was with John Edwards! She baked him a four-layer chocolate whipped cream cake anyway and decided she was going to have everyone sing happy birthday on video and send him a copy of the tape to help cheer him up. He could at least be there in spirit.

During Saturday's meeting Mary was honored with a Lifetime Membership Plaque in appreciation for all the hard work she does hosting, feeding everyone and organizing events and entertainment.

It wasn't many days before the news came that John Edwards had passed away, on Tuesday July 17th 2007. He was cremated and his ashes spread across his burned out homestead land at Lonesome Lake. With a well-hidden tear in her eye Mary told me the news. "He was the last historian, the last of the historians. I mean, who else could you say was a true historian?" she said sadly.

Frank and Claudia Cherne were down in Bella Coola one day and they noticed a sign in town that said John Edwards's Memorial Service would be held on September 29th 2007 at the Seventh Day Adventist Church at Bella Coola. Mary, Frank, and Claudia made an attempt to attend but before they even got to the summit of Heckman's Pass there was already three inches of wet snow on the road and it was really coming down fast. They took a vote and decided not to risk negotiating that winding mountainous gravel, single lane, switchback, Godforsaken Bella Coola hill and regretfully turned back and headed for home.

Mary Remembers John Edwards

As she sat in her living room, Mary began talking about John Edwards.

"We had more conversations in the past five years than in the past. I've known him since the seventies. He would come out and stop in here. I met him when I was doing the canoe trip in Tweedsmuir Park. He actually looked after that concession for the Parks on Turner Lake cuz that's where the chain is, the seven lakes. It's a famous canoeing track. Parks took it away from him in the mid-eighties I am guessing, and Tweedsmuir Lodge has it now. I don't know the politics of it but he was very upset about it all. One time we stayed in one of his cabins on Turner Lake but you did the canoe trip on your own. He rented out the cabins. He rented out the canoes too. Back then it seems to me, I thought it was about twenty dollars a day, but they tell me it's only twenty-five dollars today. He's been down there since 1912 or 1913. Terry gave him a radio, I don't know how many years ago, eight or ten years ago, and so somebody always had to answer that radio on Sunday or Wednesday. And Terry was gone a lot of times so I had to answer the radio, so I became a bit familiar with him and uh...the last five years, say for instance, he's been sick. So he's made several trips to town doing different things, especially now when he's been fighting with Parks over the fire thing, and I guess he just wanted to stop in and talk. When he came here he'd sit and talk for three hours and never stop! After a while you got tired of listening. In the moment some of it was interesting. It was always animal stuff and garden stuff, cuz they always grew a garden and lived off it. He grew everything, even fruit trees down in there at Lonesome Lake. He didn't have a freezer but he had his own little power plant. The last few years he actually, I think he's got a freezer now in the last two, three, or four years. I don't remember cuz his freezer sits over here, the freezer that he kept all his Marten food in. Terry Brandt would fly it into him. He's still got it over there. He was feedin' Foxes and Martens and everything but mostly Martens was the main thing. He would buy stuff when he went to town. It was always frozen, so then he would keep it in the freezer and every so often Terry would take him a batch of stuff down there, meat, meat stuff mmhhhmm! That's all he ever talks about is the critters, more than anything. We've seen him more this past year than any other time probably because of bein' sick and going to the hospital, having treatments and stuff. I think we only seen him twice this past year. Oh, it might have been three times. His sister is the one I talk to down in Bella Coola cuz he don't have a phone, John don't at that other cabin down at Bella Coola which is where he's staying right now I'm sure. He don't have a phone there so when I call to ask something, I ask the sister (Trudy). They seem to know what each other's doin'! But just before, to say he wasn't coming, I phoned his sister to see if he was coming to the Floatplane Association meeting and she wasn't sure. But then he did call me to say he wasn't coming the day before the meeting. Years ago, sometime during the seventies, John's sister Trudy and her husband Jack Turner bought a couple of Horses from Roger and Wanda, or Lester Dorsey, I'm not exactly sure which, from up Northeast of Anahim. They were doin' a shortcut through here. They came in on horseback and stopped for a visit. I'm not sure if I fed them lunch or not, it was so long ago. From here they went down over to the tote road below the lake which goes from Towdystan to Bella Coola down to the precipice, through the precipice to their place about a mile up the river from the old homestead. Ralph Edwards would fly in, and he'd stop in on the lake. I don't know what he was doin' whether he went to Stewart's or where he went. He always had a big garden so he brought vegetables. He stopped here. I don't know if he gave 'em to us, or if we paid for them. It was only the one time then he crashed his airplane. John flew in too, two or three times, but not a lot. He did the same thing to his plane. He landed wrong over there on Turner Lake when he was docking or something like that. I don't know if he brought vegetables or not. Just sayin' hi, going to town or something. All that is in those books, you know! The book,

'Crusoe of Lonesome Lake' will tell you all about the Edwards family. Some yo-yo stole mine! If you find the 'Crusoe of Lonesome Lake' I'd like to get it but I want the original because there's other ones. There's a Ralph Edwards book but I would have the Crusoe, that's the original, the one that was written by Leland Stowe. John's writing is mostly all to do with his critters, it's all critter stuff. What he wanted to do was put that property into a reserve, animal reserve or whatever you call it. That was what he planned to do. Whether it worked out that way or not, it's what he was doin'!" Mary explained.

Hangar Fire

During the winter of 2007 there was never really a dull moment and that fact was reinforced when the sound of explosions shattered the silence of one icy, lake-groaning, tree-cracking night. An airplane hangar fire broke out right next door to Mary's Place while her neighbors were away. A number of large exploding fuel tanks sounded like bombs going off. Massive orange fireballs shot out from the building like missiles targeting the black sky. While Logan was cutting a hole in the lake-ice to pump water to the fire, Coyotes were scattering to get away from the searing heat. If they were a bit closer when the building initially exploded they would have been fried.

In the end, efforts proved to be futile and all Mary and Logan could really do was keep out of the way of flying debris and melting metal. No amount of water was going to help so the hangar was left to burn itself out. The flames engulfed a lot of airplanes, some of which belonged to other neighbors, most of who were not insured. It burned so hot that it reduced much of the metal to molten-nothing. All that remained were crumpled, feeble looking, toothpick-like airplane frames. We were lucky that the entire area didn't burn up. It was all the snow lying around that prevented the surrounding forests from catching fire.

It was a good thing that Logan had opted not to store his newly acquired Supercub in that hangar with the other neighbor's planes. His floats were in there though, and they were vaporized. They run about twenty thousand dollars a pair. He'd left them in the hangar because his plane was on skis at the time. You could say he was one of the lucky ones.

Mary Had a Dream

The folks who own Pioneer Log Homes had some of their operations setup at the local sawmill for quite a few years and had their cabin-building plant there. Over the winters, once a week, Mary would cook up a huge pot of soup and take it to the workers. Some years before that, Brian senior had come to stay at her place for several months while Brian built Bill Bremmeyer's home down the lake.

Mary dreamed about having an even more remote wilderness cabin, more remote than the ones she had at her place. She wanted a fly-in cabin where her guests could go if they wanted to go farther out into rugged, pristine wilderness. As it happened, Brian senior possessed a deep fondness for her and had the ability to make her dream a reality, so he gave her a gift, her dream cabin.

"Brian senior stayed with Mary for a long time when they were building Bill's house. They sort-of wanted to do something for her," said Claudia Cherne. "Brian senior and Chuck, and I don't remember the names of the others who were staying there, Brian Reed who owns Pioneer Log Homes," said Frank Cherne. "Well, Tabby's husband is Brian junior, and senior was the one that stayed with Mary," said Claudia. "While they were building Bill Bremmeyer's house. That's the one that's about halfway down the lake, the big house on the left-hand side. It's a T-shaped house. If you go out to Dot Island you look straight across at it. I think it was 1995 or 1997 that it was built. They got talkin' with Nick about building a fly-out cabin somewhere. It was pretty much Nick's idea to build a remote cabin that people could fly out to," explained Frank. "Nick and Mary more or less flew around and picked out the lake up there, which is one over from Chris Czajkowski's, a seven hour hike," said Claudia. "Nick flew around until he found lakes that had a nice setting that had wild flowers and a good beach, a good place to land a floatplane. So many of the lakes have rocky shorelines and no place to land and pull a floatplane up on the beach, and that lake had a nice beach. It was a good area to build a cabin without being in an avalanche prone area. I believe the cabin was put together back in 2000. It was right around the fourth of July when we started flying the cabin up there. It was put together in four or five days. The way Pioneer Log Homes builds their homes they build 'em in their yard like they had over here by the mill. They build them, then they number all the pieces and take them apart and load them on a flatbed truck. Then they take 'em to wherever it's going to be fabricated. Well this one was built and I believe it took Mary close to two years to get authorization from Parks or from the Crown to get a lease on the land to put the cabin on. Henry, Nick, Al Maclure, Chuck, Carsten, and Brian from Pioneer Log Homes, well, Brian junior and Warren Bean and Pete Lafferty. They had Beavers, which packed a lot of stuff up. We rented a helicopter and Terry of course was up there. First of all, prior to the day of taking it up there Nick and Brian junior had all of the logs over at the log-yard over here at the mill, West Chilcotin Forest Products. Nick and myself and Henry, and a couple of other people I think helped out. But we weighed all of the logs and put them together in bundles that the helicopter could take up. And then Brian senior, Bill Bremmeyer and myself went with the truck and these bundles of logs as far out as we could drive on the roads, past Charlotte Lake out towards Cowboy Lake. We drove out as far as we could there to get as close as possible, and the helicopter would pick up a bundle of logs and take it up, drop it off up there at the cabin site, and shuttle back and forth with fifteen hundred pound bundles of logs. We slung the bundles right off the truck. They were all in bundles on the flatbed truck and the helicopter would come down with its hook and hook onto a bundle and take it up. We had all of the small pieces, all of the lumber, the tongue-n-groove for the ceiling and all of the plywood for the floor which were taken up a little at a time tied to the floats of the airplanes. It's all tied parallel to the floats, on top of the floats. The Beavers have very large flat tops on their floats so you can stack a hundred or hundred and fifty pound bundle of 2x4's, 2x10's, or 2x6's," explained Frank. "Nick had his plane loaded with plywood at one point and he couldn't get off the water. He had to come back and retie it," added Claudia. "He had to take some of it off. One winter we took up all the kitchen cabinets. They were all broken down into pieces so they could go inside of the airplane. Some of them were leftover from Bill Bremmeyer's house some that didn't fit in the house. The potty went up later," said Frank. "They flew Mary up towards the end of the project to see what was going on. She went up and spent one day up there while they were building it," said Claudia. "Chris Czajkowski hiked up the first day. Pioneer Log Homes, on their website refer to the lake where Mary's cabin was constructed as Kirner Lake but most people just call it Mary's Lake or Wilderness Lake. It's right at the foot of Wilderness Mountain about 5,600 feet up," said Frank. "That lake doesn't thaw until about the first of July. In fact, when they were building the cabin up there, there was still a big mound of ice and Pete's son brought up a friend and they had a show skidding down the ice," she said. "They were skiing up there too! It's pretty far for trekkers to get in there. It's another seven-hour hike past Chris's place. Chris's is a two-day hike from the nearest road. The best ways to get in to the cabin are either by flying or by snowmobile. Septembers are beautiful up there! The flight is about a half-hour, about thirty-five or forty miles. Chris used the cabin whenever she had people she wanted to take through," said Frank. "We usually go out at the end of July. That's usually when the wild flowers are blooming…the Lupin, Paintbrush," said Claudia holding her hand to her chest as she relived the splendor. Frank added to the list of flowers Mary loves up there. "Bog Orchids, they're a little tiny white Orchid. They're a real fragrant smelling swampy flower. The first time we stayed there was before it was completely finished, before the windows were in back in 2000. The last time we stayed there we'd been going up every year…was just this last year," he said. "Mary would figure out a menu and then we would all pitch in. We'd sit around and play cards, or fish. During the day we'd go for hikes and things because it's beautiful country," she said. "Yeah fish…or sit on the porch and watch the sun go down. When we went up there yeah, there were lots of times when I'd just fly up there for the day and clean up around the place or do things, repair work around there. I'd do everything from cleaning out the toilet to pickin' up trash that people would leave, or taking extra firewood up there. One time Henry and I went up and we drilled holes in the rocks and put in these lead anchors and pieces of chain so you'd have some place to tie the floatplanes up.

Right on the beach…yeah there were some big rocks that were just showing through the sand on the beach and we drilled into those with a hammer drill and put tie-downs so you could tie a plane up in case the wind came up in the evening. The first time we were up there, there was a pretty active storm came through and the wind was blowin' so hard it was shaking the cabin. There was just plastic stapled up over where the windows were. A gust of wind would hit and it'd be like a (Frank smacked his fist into his hand) …sounded like a bomb going off! This was in July! It passed, probably half the night. There was wind and rain when we were puttin' the cabin up! You'll see it on the video when you watch it," he said. "One of Mary's favorite spots up there is, you hike from the cabin across the little creek to where the water goes out to the little lake below. You hike across there and back and there's the falls. That's where all these wild flowers are, is in that area. That's one of her favorite places to go for a day-hike up there. We took a canoe ride once around the lake around the Itch, and that is pretty because the water is so clear. You can see right down to the bottom. They're not very big but there's fish in there. A lot of times we'd have a campfire. The creek up there had good water in it, really good water, good and cold. We'd go out and get water from there," she said. "Most of the lakes around here are either glacier or snow-fed, one of the two. That lake, there's several glaciers that feed it. Probably the third or fourth winter up there the wind was so severe it took the roof off the cabin, had to go put a new roof on. It originally had quite an overhang. It was a metal roof and the wind just peeled it back. We had to pick metal up for miles behind," he said. "But they anchored it better," she said. "They didn't put the overhang out as far," he said. After gathering up the strewn metal some of it was used for the roof on an outhouse that they later put together. It was decided that the portable potty was too messy to deal with anymore. Folks were getting sick of going in and cleaning up after people who didn't clean up after they used the cabin.

After all was built, said and done, Mary's cabin became a gorgeous getaway for her resort guests as well as for her and her friends. Pioneer Log Homes placed a page in their special project section on their web site describing some of the details about the construction of this little log-gem out in the middle of nowhere. An excerpt from their web site reads…

Mary´s Cabin

"Mary had a dream to create a get-a-way for herself and the guests of Nimpo Lake Resort. Her dream was to provide a truly natural place where her guests could fully experience the untarnished beauty of the Caribou-Chilcotin without the interruptions of everyday activity. Mary chose an uncharted area high in the mountains, accessible only by floatplane. This beautiful location, approximately 30 miles away from Nimpo Lake is now known as Kirner Lake. Kirner Lake's Elevation is 5800 feet above sea level. The ice went off the lake on June 28th, 2000, allowing the six day cabin delivery and set up to begin on July 2, 2000. Once the location was chosen, the next challenge was to provide a shelter for her guests without causing unsightly disturbances to the natural landscape. That's where Pioneer Log Homes came in. Mary's cabin was handcrafted at our Williams Lake Site then trucked to Wilderness Rim Resort at Nimpo Lake. It was then loaded piece by piece on float planes and helicopters and flown to its' new home. Involved in the remote delivery were two Beavers, a French A-Star Chopper, a Super Cub, and a 185 Cessna. In total, there were 11 Beaver Loads, 5 Chopper Loads, 15 Super Cub Loads and 45 Thermoses of Coffee hauled to the site. A team of friends and neighbors flew to the beautiful site and together set up Mary's Cabin. We would like to sincerely thank everyone who helped make Mary's dream a reality. Without these special people this project would not have been possible. Special thanks to: Pete, Warren, Wally, Al, Frank, Kay, Bryan, Tabby, Henry, Bill, Nick, and Carsten"

Table Talk

On September 2nd 2007, I sat down at the table in Mary's Loon cabin for a little morning chat with her sister Hilda while her husband went out fishing in an attempt to catch a bigger fish than she'd caught the day before. We talked a bit about what it was like for her and Mary growing up. "I was born in 1942 and my dad sold-out in 1954. He had froze his hands so many times that the cold weather in winter was really starting to bother him. A young guy from Saskatchewan who lived maybe three or four miles away, he and my dad kind of worked together a little bit. He had a few Cattle. I can almost remember him comin' for dinner. And my dad said if anybody ever came and offered him ten thousand dollars he'd sell-out. So this kid wrote his dad and pretty soon his dad was out there and offered my dad ten thousand dollars cash. My dad sold the place in Goodwin. From Goodwin we went to Grande Prairie, it's a big city now. Then my dad came to BC, went down to Aldergrove and bought property and he got a job working for the railroad. I think we sold-out in the fall and we were there all winter 'til spring. He went away for six months to work, then he came back and got us and we moved out there from Grande Prairie to Aldergrove. He had bought ten acres.

There were these two young guys who worked for my dad (in Goodwin) that were like brothers to me. I mean, if they'd come along and they were haying or something, I was gone with them. One guy died a couple years ago. All through my life I missed them. When we moved to the coast I thought maybe I'd marry one of 'em. I hated it at the coast because there was nothing for us kids to do anymore. I tried to run away three or four times but I didn't get very far. But then they went to Europe to work on those communication-tower things on the mountains. Growing up with these two guys, they were only ten years older than me. One was Clyde Crowe and the other was Billy Thew. His mother came from Tatla Lake. She was a schoolteacher there. I guess she had advertised it in the paper and Billy's dad just got out of the war somehow and they got together there. I was born in Billy Thew's mom and dad's house in Grande Prairie. His grandfather had an old second hand store. That's where I was born because the hospital had the measles. Babies and measles don't mix. The older we got I always used to say to my mother, why didn't you name me Rose? You know, I could be 'Second Hand Rose' in that song ya know! I think Mary was born in the hospital. dad would work with other people, together doing other people's haying. People would help each other out all the time. My dad had a thrashing machine. They didn't, so he'd take the thrasher over to thrash their fields and he'd been gone it seemed to me only a couple days but to think back it seemed like it was a week. So we were happy to see him come home. He had the tractor, the thrashing machine and in behind there had the Horses and the wagon. And in behind there, more Horses and another wagon. Mary and I, well we went to climb up on the wagon. He'd opened the gate to drive the tractor and the thrashing machine through. He didn't know we were getting on the back of the hay wagon. Anyhow, Mary made it, I didn't! When he jerked the tractor I fell down and the next wagon and Horses ran over me. I couldn't get up but Mary ran into the house. Mother, she'd come out and ran to the neighbors. I don't know how she got there. I have no idea whether she took one of the Horse teams or not, I don't know. And they come in an old Model-A car to get me. One of those old square things, you know. We headed for Grande Prairie, which is about 35 miles now. I remember bein' in the hospital and I screamed and I screamed. And they wouldn't take me out with the kids. I don't know if I was in pain. I remember laying in the bed and bein' flat and couldn't get up. Nobody ever told me what I broke. It wasn't 'til the family reunion that they finally told me about my broken pelvis. In the hospital, it was funny, I got moved into the nurse's station. The doctor came to see me. Why he would'a give me a stick of gum I don't know but he gave me gum. I had long hair and I'd gotten that gum all through my hair. I can still hear those nurses mad at that doctor. I was about eight years old. It seems I was there a whole month or something. It was a long time. You know the brush and willows, like you know how they've got the rows. They'd cut it all off and Mary fell off a Horse one day and got one of those sticks poked in her neck. Put a hole in. Mary and I, we shared a double bed when we were kids in Goodwin and maybe for a little bit in Grande Prairie. I remember one time her and I were fightin' and we broke a window in the new house my dad built in 1951. Dad came home and he was mad. We crawled under the bed so he couldn't reach us. He said we were lucky he couldn't. Sometimes we used to wear flour sacs for dresses but most of the time our clothes came out of the Free-Press-Weekly, that old farmer's magazine. In the back you could get clothes. At the time I thought they might have been used because you'd get a cotton dress that was kinda faded but maybe that was the style. Musta got the shoes that way too. But the flour sacs were white with some kinda thing written on them. In the summer I can't remember wearing too much for clothes. Shorts, but never no top and no shoes. I can remember my mother up until she died, never wore shoes in the house. In the wintertime she'd go outside, no shoes on. I think my dad wished I'd been born a boy because he always had me do a lot of the heavy outside work. I used to feed fifteen or twenty Pigs, and milk ten Cows. I'd help my mother milk 'em, feed the Chickens, all before I went to school. Mary was in the house getting' breakfast, making bread or something. I'm sure she made bread at ten years old. She never had to milk or clean the barns or nothin'. I think, because my mother worked so much on the farm, I can't remember her ever on a tractor but she always had the Horses. She could harrow with the Horses and my dad would be on the tractor ploughin'. My mother always did seem to have time to cook. She was a good cook, but she did a lot of outside work. My dad had missin' fingers. He stuck them in a buzz saw. He couldn't milk but then my mother did all that stuff when she was home too. Her two sisters, I don't think did too much at home. I don't know if her brother had gone to war. He lost his eye before he went to war. He lost it with a pitchfork. But I think my mother did a lot of the outside work at that time and she did a lot of trapping. Mother was a hunter and trapper. The photo of the woman sitting on the Moose is my mom. She shot the Moose and that was her brother sitting beside her. When we were kids mother used to trap on the Smokey

116

River. We used to follow her in the wintertime. She got Beaver and Muskrat, and Weasels. I can still remember helping hold that stinkin' Weasel, Marten, you know you skin 'em out and those scent glands are worse than a skunk. I had to hold 'em while she was skinning them out. Then you'd tie 'em on that board ya know, tie their feet up there and dry 'em, the skins. I used to hate to hafta cut the heads off the Chickens but I would not. They would maybe have had to beat me to do it but I would not clean the Chickens, that was Mary's job. To this day I've never ate a Chicken leg. I'll eat Chicken breast, same with the Turkey. I won't eat anything else. I think that goes back to cuttin' the heads off. I had a, what would you call it, a space between my front teeth. I used to eat beef and it would get hung-up there. So I got so when I was a kid I would never eat any meat. I'd just stick it under the table, hold it in my hand to feed the Dog, because at that time there were no toothpicks. You take a look at those old corn brooms and that was what we used to have for toothpicks. I don't think it was really that dirty but at the time I used to hate to have to pick that corn broom apart to get a toothpick. I never ate much meat 'til Norm and I got together and got married. We raised our own. When you're on a farm like that you've got lots of cream eh, eggs and milk sort of thing, butter. Mom was very good at making angel food cake, cream puffs, jelly rolls. I remember those three things and to this day I still don't want to look at 'em. Seen and ate too much of it I guess. Mary learned a lot of that stuff on her own I think. I'd always help my dad in the fields. I'd be pickin' weeds, wild oats out of the Barley and Wheat fields, stinkweed. It was always that way. I remember my first trip back out there to Alberta ten years ago. My daughter was out there working for a farmer. She was in there helping him raise the Pigs. But I walked out in his fields and I could still name all the weeds that we had in Grande Prairie, well Edgewood, where we lived. If you take those words and mix them up a little bit, it spells good weed. I don't know if it was four years ago or so here, but the Beavers plug up the creek every once in a while. Mary went out there to work at it, clean it up, and be dammed if the Beaver didn't plug it again. So now it was serious, they had to get rid of the Beaver. So Connie was here. I think Niko was a baby. Anyhow, she cooked it up just to try it, skinned it out and was gonna try it, and we came along. She said to Norm, you

117

wanna try that Beaver with me and Norm said, sure. So she went and roasted it and they tried it for supper but it was pretty tough. I would think you'd have to boil the hell right outta the Beaver and then roast it, marinate it or something." Explained Hilda vividly remembering every detail.

As Hilda and I sat chatting Mary came walkin' up the steps of the Loon cabin and pulled up a chair and started right in with a story about sneakin' around in the cornfield, smoking cigarettes. "We never had paper. Dad had tobacco because he used to smoke a pipe, but we never had paper to roll a cigarette in and we were only fourteen, fifteen, or thirteen whatever, twelve, I don't remember! So we used newspaper and rolled it up and we'd go hide in between the rows of corn," explained Mary. "Cecile Alan's daughter, what was her name Kaye? They were over with the little one! The three of us smoked. Kaye, you and I! We got pukin' outside there and mother put all three of us to bed. She thought we had the flu but it was the smokin' that did it," said Hilda. "Actually, we hardly did it," said Mary as Hilda looked at her analytically. "I've smoked since! I don't know how you started. You started with somebody at school," Hilda replied. "No, my first boyfriend Jim Closson," argued Mary. "No, it was before that!" Hilda argued back. "Well anyhow, we were still up there so when we moved down there I was still sixteen eh, fourteen?" said Mary. "No, we'd already been on the farm," replied Hilda. "But anyhow I don't remember. I did smoke a little, but then I met Jim Closson and he thought that was terrible. I quit smokin' right then! I'd hardly started. Tell me where we coulda got our cigarettes from. I have no idea!" asked Mary. "I don't know and I was alone with you and you had a couple friends and that's how I got smokin'. They were in school and it was out by the outhouse!" replied Hilda. "That's one thing today you hear, they're not gonna smoke in the schoolyards anymore. That's all finished. Now they'll have to go further out in the street or something," said Mary. "Ya, they'll be makin' 'em late for school!" replied Hilda.

Down Goes Another and Another

During the month of August 2007 there was a man visiting Nimpo from the United States and he was flying around in his plane practicing landing on the water to get his float experience hours up. The day was quite windy and he might have been hit by a gust. He plowed his plane into the shore destroying one of his floats. Somehow or another he must have misjudged the depth of the water near the shoreline or hit a tail wind and had gotten himself pushed sideways. He ended up putting his plane down with one float on the gravel and one in the water. He was uninjured but was a little peeved at himself and maybe a bit embarrassed that he'd gotten into such a spot on the beach.

Logan, Frank Cherne, and a couple other guys took a boat over to the plane to assess how, not if, it could be brought back over to the Mary's neighbor's dock. Then they could trailer it over to Frank's hangar to get a new float on. After a few days of pacing around all hours of the night rolling physics around in their brains Frank and Logan came up with the idea to untie one of Mary's docks and tow it over to the plane. They took several barrels and filled them with water then sank the barrels down to where they could be positioned under the damaged float, which was under water. Then they let the water out and filled the barrels with air to buoy them up under the float. They tied the plane to the dock and ferried the plane back over. It was an amazing feat but out in the wilderness when something like that happens you do what you gotta do. Ain't nobody gonna come rescue a plane way out here for less than a zillion dollars.

As bad luck would have it, the pilot forgot to turn off his emergency locator transmitter after his accident so he left it on for hours just a-beeping away. That brought the search and rescue onto the scene, flying over Mary's Place, a yellow Buffalo airplane from CFB Comox. Mary had her eye on the goings-on across the lake, standing at the window with Claudia Cherne, lookin' over there just in case they needed her for something. The guys were over working on the bent plane when the Buffalo went overhead. At some point the guys must have communicated with the Buffalo because after a few minutes it turned and headed off into the distance. Mary and Claudia looked at each other shaking their heads wondering why the heck three pilots were right there and not one of them thought of turning off the ELT.

When they finally got that wrecked plane over to the dock Mary ran over and grabbed the rope they tied on and started pulling that darn thing out of the water and up the ramp. There's nothing that woman won't do!

"Wayne was the one that called me and I told him what happened out there and he says ah they need to turn off their ELT (emergency locator transmitter). And so when I talked to Frank I called Mary and told her, if Frank is still down there have him tell them to turn off the ELT, cuz he was going back over there," said Claudia Cherne. "Yeah that's one of the things he should have done instinctively as soon as it hit. But he and Logan were out there and I took a quad around and hiked through the bush," said Frank. "And of course the speaker thing fell out and it quit making the noise but it was still broadcasting cuz it hadn't been turned off, see," added Claudia. "Normally you go and check to see if the ELT is going by turning on your aircraft radio. Well there was fuel leaking out so everything was turned off. Nobody would turn anything on, take a chance of an explosion and a fire. He didn't think of turning it off when he hit," explained Frank as he went on to describe how they rigged up a plan to get the plane out. "We built a raft over there and with two fifty five gallon drums, sunk them, put it down under the spreader bars. Then floated the plane. Then we pumped the water out of them and that gave enough floatation to lift the plane up off the bottom. We made a plug to go in the drum with a piece of plastic going into the bottom of the drum. Had a piece of garden hose for a vent that came out and was up above the water. So we could pump the water out and the

120

garden hose would let air into the drum. Then we tied some big planks across the spreader bars and over to the dock, so that if those happen to have come loose while we were in the middle of the lake we wouldn't lose the airplane. So the dock and the airplane went as one unit for safety. He was really lucky there. If it had been to one side of the float a little bit and didn't hit the float, it would've taken the wing off. And if it had been the other side of the float and would hit between it would've gotten the engine and the prop. So he was pretty lucky where it happened to hit!" he said. "The same day that the other plane crashed out here his mechanic flew in," said Claudia. "Yeah another plane out on the runway out here flipped upside down. A guy from Hundred-Mile," said Frank. "That was the day Mary was working at the post office last Wednesday. Wayne from the airport called and said there was a fella gonna come in and land here on the runway. He thought he was more familiar with it. Well he landed the wrong way. The one (runway) that's x'ed off which is not to be used, he landed there and ended up going into a ditch and flipped the plane over," said Claudia. "It was a Citabria, the other plane was a Mahl. The guy and a friend and his daughter were with him and when he hit he sort-of bumped his head. His glasses cut the bridge of his nose. There was some blood from his nose, the bridge of his nose being cut, but the plane was taken apart and Duke Sager hauled it out, hauled it back to Hundred-Mile," said Frank. "Well anyway the same day that this happened the other guy's mechanic flew in on the afternoon skid. The guy brought him here and they were looking at his plane here while we were trying to take care of the other situation. But his mechanic said no, there was just too much damage to try and fly it out," said Claudia. "When it hit, there was so much weight with all the fuel in the wings, caused some damage up where the wings attach. There was some bent tubing up there so that it was pretty obvious at the time but I left it to his mechanic to give him the bad news. I'm not an aircraft mechanic. Then he drove down to Washington and picked up his wheels. We took the floats off. He took them into Springhouse where a guy is gonna repair the floats," said Frank. "It's going to have to be trailered out," added Claudia. "The plane is out in my hangar!" said Frank.

Accolades

William Graham, known as Bill, has visited the Nimpo area all the way from Seeley Lake, Montana, nearly every year for the past 47 years. He first brought his wife Virginia, known as Ginny, who is now passed away, to Nimpo Lake back in 1970. He recounts some of his experiences and thoughts about Mary during his 47th visit in September 2006, while he was tenting with his son Dwayne.

"I found out about this place in 1958. My dad's boss was up here in '58. Dad had always wanted to take me somewhere to catch some decent fish, instead of those little hatchery things. So we camped here in 1959. It took us thirteen hours from Williams Lake to here, Nimpo Lake. That's only driving time, that's not stoppin' and breakin' and overnight. It took us two days when we had overnight at Bull Canyon. The roads was so rough and it just beat your hands to pieces. It was low in second gear. If you were goin' twenty-five you were speedin'. It wasn't paved at all, in fact in 1959, it was the last year we went over the old suspension bridge over the Fraser River. Then it was 1960 when they built the cement bridge over the Fraser down at the bottom of Sheep's Crik hill, and it was rough, rough, rough from Williams Lake, washboard way up over the hill and down the other side. The only smooth on the whole road was when ya cross the bridge. Then you went up Sheep's Crik hill, which was treacherous, narrow, and lots of curves and you went up, and up, and up. Then once you get on top to Risky Crik, then we'd go across Meldon Prairie which was loaded with rocks, rougher 'en a cob! Big, big rocks ya know? You better hope you got a couple spare tires with ya! Now, there were places along the way where you could get tires fixed. Ahh Puntzi Lake, Alexis Crik, ah Redstone. I think even at one time Risky Crik had a place you could get a tire fixed. Most every settlement, you could get a tire changed! We always came up in the summer. The only time we ever ran into snow was now, in 2006, where we're having a nice little snowstorm in September! It's cold, but it's alright! In 1970 when my wife and I came and it was the first time for her. Never had a fishin' pole in 'er hand in her life, never been campin' in her life! So we stayed in a cabin, cabin #1. Her first fish, it was hilarious! She was lettin' her line out. We were trollin' and all of a sudden I told her to be prepared for the line goin' down because the spools are doin' all kinda weird things cuz there's no tension on it see! We were fishin' for Rainbow Trout. Her first one was about nineteen inches and it weighed about two pounds. That was Sunday. I couldn't get 'er to stop by Friday! She fished 'til ten, eleven o'clock at night. We came up on in 1974 in a 1956 Robins-egg-blue Volkswagen. After my mother passed away we brought a green and yellow Ford crew cab pick-up! We had my three kids, my wife, and my dad, plus two Dogs. Used to drive from Montana, nine hundred and fifty miles to come up here. Now, it's very hard because there are so many memories, so many memories! My wife loved Mary like a sister! Mary is just a one-of-a-kind lady. I can't explain it. She's outgoing, well she's just like a mother takin' care of all 'er kids. It's just the way it is! I brought my son Dwayne up here for his first visit back in about nineteen and seventy-one (1971). He used to play with Mary's son Robert. He loved to play with Robert, ya. You could take him (Dwayne) out fishin'. He really didn't want to fish and he'd be catching all the fish. And we're trying to catch fish and he'd be screwin' around in the boat and all that. His pole was catching fish right and left. We'd catch an odd one here and there but he was catchin' most of 'em, ya know, beautiful fish! We knew all of Mary's kids. Clark, Connie, and Robert. In fact in 1970 I went and picked them up from the school bus with their motorbike, a little putt-putt. When asked if he ever observed the boys picking on Mary's only daughter Connie, Bill said, "No, oh no, she's a pretty scrappy kid, oh yah very tough, very tough, very strong! She just loves the place like her mother does. She loves the wild and ah no people, and just like I do in Montana. Right off the bat when I met Mary, I could tell that this lady was gonna go somewhere. She is one of a million as far as a host. She don't treat you like you're a customer. You're one of her kids, and you come to visit once a year! It's just the way, she's a gracious host. She bends over backwards to give ya the best time. She's always putin' in stuff and not chargin', all this kinda stuff. She would do all this baking and just give it to ya. She wouldn't sell it to ya. All this bread and rolls, oh she gave it all away you know? I remember staying in the cabins for eight dollars a day until Mary and Elvin (Mary's then-partner) took the place over. Then the boat went with the cabin, eight bucks a day! That's why you didn't drag a boat in here cuz the roads was so rough it'd beat it to pieces. When we're campin' Mary will come walkin' down, usually carryin' sumthin to eat. She's just that way. She loves her job afterall she's been here about thirty-eight years yah. I let Mary smoke my fish. She hangs the fish up cuz you hafta dry the slime off of 'em. Then she splits 'em down the backbone with heads on cuz that's the Canadian law. In case the game warden wants to check the length, he can do it. Then she sprinkles a little salt on with 'er hand and sprinkles on a little brown sugar. Then she puts them in 'er smoker, which is a big thing with about four racks and she smokes 'em for about eight to nine hours. You want green wood because you want the smoke. You don't want too much heat cuz you don't wanna cook 'em yah yah. She's usin' Aspen or Birch, whatever you want to call it. It's a leafy wood you know. It's a leafy tree. Gotta be green! You can't use Pine 'er you'd ruin 'em. You couldn't eat 'em. We've got pictures of Indians and their wagons and for-real cowboys out herdin' their Cattle. I remember Lenny and Mary Lemke built their cabin in nineteen and fifty-five. I think he died on this lake fishin'," said Bill as he poured himself a steaming hot cup of campfire coffee.

"There are lots of things I like about my mom," said Mary's daughter Connie. "When I think of all the things she's taught me in life, she's taught me what I consider to be very valuable lessons. As far as how we see ourselves as human beings and how to treat other people and animals...in fact, all living things! Three words that I can use to describe my mom...would be kind, caring, and compassionate. She's kind in many ways. Her kindness and respect for animals has been a good experience and learning lesson for me. She taught me that all animals needed to be treated kindly, fairly, and with compassion. You don't abuse animals. You make sure they're fed and have a warm home. Dogs deserve extra blankets in their Doghouses and Chickens get extra hay in the Chicken house.

You make them comfortable and treat them well emotionally and psychologically. You make sure they don't suffer and are well fed and when they get sick you take them to the vet. I think her animals have always known how much she loved them by the way she cared for them. On the other hand when an animal is no longer useful, for example our Cows...one got sick from a little bit of milk-fever and wasn't able to recoup from that, the animal was butchered and put on the table. My mom has always shown excitement or kind regards towards all living things. She's often told me that if you look hard enough you'll find the good in everybody and every thing. She is always thinking about other people and doing things for them to make them happy, to show them that someone, she, does genuinely care. People from all walks of life, it doesn't matter who. She's always had a hot meal for somebody, a steaming cup of coffee, a warm bed, and a burning hearth, you know! The fire would always be on and the house warm. She gives unconditionally to her community. She would often cook for public gatherings or she would work tirelessly in the hot summer sun to sell rodeo tickets, and she would donate generously to others. In particular, she has a favorite donation that she likes to do. The Variety Club telethon... She is so eager every year when the time comes for the community to get together and have their auction for the telethon. And that just really makes her happy. She loves to help sick children. She was rewarded for this a few years ago. The community presented her with a really nice bench for her kindness and selfless giving to the community. I'm very proud of her for that. She was a foster parent in my early childhood. She would have children into her home and look after them when they had been abused and taken out of their own homes. I remember some of these kids. I recall one child in particular. A mentally challenged young child in her home and she had placed him and me in the same crib. We were both probably about two years old. I remember that child biting me very hard. My mom said, what saddened her most about that job was that the children would be returned to their homes when in fact the home hadn't really been given the resources or the ability to change and become a better home and it wouldn't be better for the children. She often saw them going back to the same circumstances from which they came. One time she also foster-parented a young boy who was half-Native, half-Caucasian. He was considered a hard-to-place child. My mother absolutely fell in love with him. He was a chubby little baby always happy, content, and just had the best personality in the world. So she decided to adopt him. That's how we came about getting my younger brother (Robert). I too was adopted. Once again, my mom found that another child needed a home and she wanted a daughter. She always presented my adoption to me as, my biological mother had given me up because she loved me enough to give me a better home. And I think that was the strongest, best message she could have given me. She fostered the feelings of goodness so there would be no anger. It was just a really good way for her to put it! I'm glad she adopted me. She's taught me so much. I just think she's been the greatest. I don't think I could have been adopted to a better mother! My mom feels that there are far too many unwanted children in this world. She is definitely pro-adoption! She often suggests that if people want a child they should consider adopting one. I have one particular memory when years and years ago as a child we had a fellow, an older man come in on a Horse. He was an old cowboy and he'd been riding in the bush for about a month and he hadn't had a bath. He was just as dirty as could be, but you know mom had dinner cooked and she made sure that he sat down at the table and made sure that he got a full meal and lots to drink. It didn't matter to her what he looked like or what he might have smelled like. She was completely hospitable showing him that she truly cared. And I could tell from his face and his actions that he appreciated everything she'd done for him. I've seen a great deal of passion throughout my mom's life for flowers. She absolutely loves flowers and plants. She seems to glow in the wonder of a tiny little seed turning into a huge mass vibration of color, you know? I see her the most passionate when we are walking through the mountains and there's a large dark gray rock and she'll find a little tiny sprinkle of pink flowers amidst nothing else but gray rock. She's just amazed that that little thing came out and was able to survive and do so well in that place. It never seems to wane. She has a wonder and awe for just about any flower that she sees, particularly those that are found in places you don't often find them. She has a passion for nature. She sees our society as growing too large and taking more of the Earth's surface, leaving less area for the wild animals to live on. She has strong feelings about unnecessarily killing wild animals, that there are so few of them left now and wonders if our grandchildren will have to go to a zoo to see them. So when people go out just for the sport of killing she understands killing for food and mercy but not for the sport. She's been known to many times speak about that. She's also passionate about hard work and accountability. I remember her saying you work hard before asking for any help from anybody else. You work as hard as you can to help yourself. You work your fingers to the bone before you ask for welfare. She's always lived her life that way and very rarely ever asked anything of others, and yet she's always giving. I think that taught me a valuable lesson, working hard for myself. It's taught me that I'm able and capable, and can be happy with myself and with what I have to offer the world. Another thing my mom has taught me is that, if you can't say something nice about somebody don't say anything at all. And I remember when I was a kid and she'd tell me that. I just didn't understand the concept. I didn't see what the big deal was but I heard it over and over and over again. Not in response to me saying something ...but it's just something she'd say once in a while. As an adult I have really come to understand that concept. What I've learned in my life is that when somebody does something bad nobody forgets. Whenever somebody does something good nobody remembers. Whenever you decide you're only going to say something nice about a person whatever you say is going to come back to you to some degree. When you decide to say something bad about somebody it's usually a reflection, wanting to make yourself feel better. And this is not a healthy way to live life. My mom always tries to think happy thoughts, feeling that we have control over our lives because our happiness comes from our own minds. I've grown up watching her work hard and tirelessly, and it's always amazed me seeing her basically doing all the running of the resort, all the cabin cleaning, making sure everybody had boats and worms to go fishing with. And she'd be bakin' bread, kneading, rolling and rising...all kinds of bread and buns. She'd send me up the hill to all the campers and cabins with armloads of oven-warm homemade bread. Often she would send along a little homemade butter and I remember helping make that butter. We'd make sour cream into a gallon jar and we'd shake and shake it. That was one of our jobs. We took turns shaking it. Ten minutes each. Pretty soon it turned into a big lump of homemade butter. That is one of the reasons people keep coming back 40 years later. They remember that homemade bread and down-home hospitality, mom's kindness and sincerity! At the end of a really long hard day she'd go down to the barn and milk herself three Cows and bring home two big buckets of milk. She always made sure the Cats in the barn and lots of warm milk and she'd bring home her milk and she'd have sterilized jars all ready. She'd pour the milk into the jars and I'll tell ya that cream on top of that milk. The thickness was incredible. You could cut it with a knife. it was the thickest most delightful cream. She'd sell that milk and it was in such high demand. Always when we had company over we had lots of that to put on the dessert. Mom swears to this day that it was all the fresh milk and Chicken eggs that kept us as healthy as we are. Then after the milking she'd be putting her rubber boots on and bouncing off into the bush to the creek and she'd start pulling apart the Beaver dams. And there she'd be up to her knees in flowing ice-cold water yanking big sticks out of the dam. Those Beavers know how to build intertwining all the sticks. She'd come home just full of dirt and grit. Then she'd go have herself a bath and call it a day. It amazes me and she still does it to this day, how she loves to cut firewood, chainsaw in hand, just roaring away. She gets someone else to drop the trees for her but boy she gets in there and cuts off each branch and then cuts the whole tree up into pieces just the right size. She takes all the branches and puts them in a pile and burns them… nice high hot fire. And then she rolls the cut-up-logs where they need to be put, then she rakes in the fire. That was one of her little chores for the day and she thinks nothing of it. It's just an incredible amount of work. It's the kind of work so many women would never want to do, or consider, or never had the opportunity to do. Running a chainsaw and cutting up a tree. These experiences are such a norm for her, when in fact it is not actually normal to me, it's incredible! When people came over for an evening visit it was not unusual for mom to take ten-minute catnaps. People just knew that she went to sleep for ten minutes in her chair, woke right up again and jumped up to make sure everybody had cookies or cake. She'd be so tired out but she sprang back so fast. It's what I call the German-stock. Her dad did the same thing, work hard, work hard, work hard. I remember him, eighty years old, throwing hay on a pitchfork, working tirelessly in the sun. I think it was genetic but also something that was taught. Mom doesn't believe in wasting anything. You reuse plastic bags, paper, and clothing. Not a speck of food goes into the garbage. It ends up in the Chicken dish. She made sure everyday that the Chickens got lots of table scraps and goodies. I think it was this last winter or the one before there was this big Moose hind quarter on the lake. So she hollered to Logan to go down and get that Moose leg. It's such a waste, all that meat. Why leave it on the lake when you can make roasts and steaks and give to the elders. There is always somebody hungry out there. We figure that one of the hunters probably lost it off their sled going across the lake. So Logan brought it home and it was frozen solid. Mom put that Moose leg on her back porch and it sat there for a couple of days and she looked at it thinking of all kinds of things she could do. I don't know what she finally did with it. But I know she didn't waste it! That's what my mom is all about!" explained Connie.

Their first family Cow was named Twiggy. The logic behind the name was that old farmer had found her roaming around abandoned in the bush, twig-thin. Connie was full of excitement as Mary took her down a hot, dirty road to buy Twiggy. When they arrived at the old farmer's place, they were greeted with homemade pea soup. The old man's face was tanned and leathered from so many years of gathering hay...which is no easy job. That job causes a person to do a lot of squinting, as many outdoor jobs do when you face the bright sun at a high altitude. The old farmer had fattened Twiggy-up to increase her value for the sale. Later on, Mary borrowed another neighbor's Bull, which subsequently fattened Twiggy-up even more and resulted in this sweet white pet Cow giving birth to twin calves. The next few years seemed to repeat itself with Twiggy bringing forth more sets of twins. She seemed to gain girth each time around, a girth that never reduced. So Twiggy grew so wide she could barely fit through the barn door and the time came when not-so-little Twiggy could no longer squeeze through at all. When I asked what became of her, she displayed a little side-grin and replied, "What do you think?" So Twiggy steak was on the menu for a while after that. Connie recalled a particularly tasty favorite, Twiggy sausage!

Another Cow named Laurie came down with some kind of infection in her milk udder. So Mary set-up a hoist system in the barn and lifted that Cow right up into the air to get her off her feet. This was an attempt to rectify the problem but to no avail and Laurie had to be put-down. This time I never asked what they did with the meat.

Mary always tried to keep a steer for food in the fall and a few Cows for milking. Interestingly, she doesn't drink milk and claims only to have drank one glass when she was in the hospital giving birth to her son Clark, just to satisfy the nurses. She always named her Cows after people. Her daughter Connie recalls that one was named after a large, mean lady. But she refused to name the woman due to the risk of identifying that person in public and possibly hurting her feelings. But she didn't shy away from saying that the physical and personality attributes of that Cow matched the woman pretty well. When asked about the Cow, Mary stated very clearly that naming her after the woman had nothing whatsoever to do with her and was more something the kids decided to do. "It was Connie's doin'!" said Mary firmly. But Connie claims it wasn't her doing either, that it was the neighbor's doin'. It would be safe to say that no one will ever know or admit whose doin' it was.

"I've known Mary since about 1979," said Val King, one of Mary's longtime friends. "We bought our place it was 1977 and I met her when I came up in the summers when we were building the house, but 1980 was when I arrived here to stay. I knew her pretty much from then on. I think Mary's daughter Connie and my daughter are about the same age so they went to school together up here. Mary's son Clark I didn't know too well. Her son Robert, I knew him. I can't remember Clark too much. Mary is about the only one, I would say she's well rounded. She's out there for everybody. She helped people and never wanted anything in return. She didn't like surprises, you know she didn't want you to do anything for her. We did things for her once in a while whether she liked it or not. I could see what type of person she was pretty much right away. A few years back Anita Madson had sort of a surprise-appreciation for her at Anahim Resort. They had a little plaque made for her, for doing so many things for people. I don't think she was too happy about it. She's gone to the mill with me sometimes and helped me get the short ends of the leftover wood and things. She's helped me a lot. She's got more ambition for doing things than some men. I don't know how they (the men) accept that. I think they just know hey that's Mary and don't bother trying to do anything about it. They just let her do her thing. She was a substitute teacher at the school years ago for kindergarten all the way up. We'd have progressive dinner parties and we'd go around to different houses and have an entree at each place. We'd start out at one house having a cocktail and appetizers. That must have been in the 80's. We'd go to Frank and Betty Ayers's house. And a lot of the different schoolteachers that are gone now, we'd go to their houses. Diane Chamberland, she's still the secretary at Anahim Lake School. We couldn't go to my house because I lived at the ranch and it was too far away. We'd get a group of maybe ten people. And at one house there'd be the cocktails. The second house would be appetizers. We'd pick that person up and go onto the next place then end up at the last house where the main course was and that's where the party would be. It was fun! Then we'd have Box Socials at Nimpo Lake Hall where the ladies would make dinners. We'd wrap them (the dinners) in tablecloths or whatever and the guys would bid on them. They didn't know whose dinner they were buying and they'd have dinner with the person who cooked it. Then we'd have a dance afterwards. They were paying up to seventy or eighty dollars for a meal. We'd also have pie-socials where the ladies made pies. Mary did that because she was such a great pie-maker, a great cook period! And the guys would bid on the pies to raise money for the hall, Nimpo Lake Hall. We'd just have a big party after that. So whoever wanted to come just made pies. All the ladies made pies and the guys bid on them. Mary took me to her wilderness cabin for the weekend one year for my birthday, one year, and that was fun. Gideon flew us out there. There was Mary, Frank and Claudia, and a bunch of us. I think there were six of us. Then a bunch of pilots flew in the next day. Chris Czajkowski trekked in from her place. It was great you know Mary loves to dance. Her and I would dance together at dances. The guys wouldn't ask because we'd get up and dance. We had a good time. Mary would go grab them and pull them up on the dance floor. They wouldn't say no! Yah, just remember lots of good times.

We're sort of trying to revitalize things cuz you know I find people are getting stale. We're not doing, maybe it's age related, but I don't feel my age so why should we stop doing things? So, we're trying to do, we had the auction at Nimpo Lake Hall. We had a New Year's dance. You know Mary loves anything like that too! I think I only ever missed one or two of Mary's dances through all the years she had them. She's has always been a very positive person. I mean even if there was umm not a nice situation she always seemed to make a good situation out of it. You know nothing was negative. She found the good out of whatever the situation was. Yah that's Mary you know! Sometimes you'd get a little, you know, come-on Mary you gotta admit things are bad sometimes! But she wouldn't give in. With our birthdays we'd always usually have lunches. She'd put on lunches. The one year that stopped she said she'd rather people put the money toward the Variety Club or Children's Hospital, which makes sense. You know we don't need anything so why just buy a gift for the sake of buying a gift? The person just puts it in a drawer and never uses it or gives it to someone else. So I said that was great because I don't believe in giving gifts. You know I get together with the girls to celebrate someone's birthday, have a drink or lunch and um you know I stuck to it but the odd time people are still bringing gifts. Mary needed a man in her life and I'm glad she found one who is compatible. She wanted a man in her life for a companion. She wasn't too happy on her own. She had roughly six years on her own before she met Logan," recalled Val.

"Bill and I retired up here in 2001, Before that we were seasonal. We've had our cabin since 1983. That's a long time we've been coming up here! And we used to go to Mary's parties every summer. Mary went out of her way to make us feel welcome when we retired here," said Joan Smiley. "Bill knew more people because he was up all the time throughout the year workin' on the cabin, whereas I just came at Easter and in the summer and Thanksgiving. We met Mary through Rollie. He brought us down to one of her parties, the barbeque things, the dance. She always did the pit-thing you know, smoked all her meat and had the canoe and pop. Before we came up here we never snowmobiled before. I love it! We've snowmobiled down the lake quite a few times this year but we haven't driven. Only once have I driven! Yah the lake wasn't good for driving this year. We went to Reno when we first started building the cabin. There was Rollie and Patty, Frank and Betty, ahh Mary and Nick, Bill and I, and then one of the cops and his wife. We went to Reno for New Years. We knew Mary but I mean we've only really become friends in the last umm five or six years that we've been retired. And it was thanks to her that I made friends in the community because I didn't really know anybody here when we retired. I never came up in the winter. She made a point of including us in anything that was happening...yah. Every Tuesday we have nacho day, nachos and chile. Since we retired up here I got to be included in it but her and Lois used to do it all the time. Mary said "Well, if you wanna come you know I won't be phonin' ya every week!" So I came! She made us feel welcome. The men are not included! In the summer it's usually a little busier. Maxine usually goes for lunch when she's here. She lives up the first road. They're old timers. When Claudia and Florence are here they go too. We have our nachos and have a glass of wine and yah. In the summers Mary is so busy but she says "I have to stop for lunch, so!" She's one in a million! I stopped and looked at her new little Llama on my way in here. He's a little cutie! We went to Branson with Mary two years ago. She arranged it of course, arranged all the shows, which she knew what shows were good to go to. We went to shows every day we were there. We were there a week. Mary and I did three shows for a couple of days. It's all country music. We saw the Oakridge Boys, Mel Tillis, ahh Mickey Gilly. When we went it was just Mary, Logan, and Bill and I and it was at the start of the season, like in May. So it was pretty quiet there, just gettin' goin' in Branson. But we had a good time. In the winter we would go to the Chilcotin Gate restaurant for dinner once a week. And now we have our burger night on Saturdays. One week Mary does it and one week we do it, then one week Frank and Betty do it! Because there was no restaurant this last winter. And there's a poker night on Friday night at Len's shop for the guys. That's my night off. I used to see Mary coming across the lake on her snowmobile bringing fresh milk from her Cows to Pine Point Resort. She had the milk in a big glass thing! She's just a wonderful person! If Mary wasn't here this place would be an empty void! She's just part of the country! She's done a lot for the community of Anahim and Nimpo. Not this last year but the year before at the Anahim Hall Mary kept after Bill all night you know. There's this good prize coming!" And it was all nicely wrapped in a nice big box and she kept after Bill to bid on this. And it was close to the end (of the Variety Club fundraiser auction. He's bidding and she's after him to bid, bid, bid! Bill and Len are bidding against each other. And you know it got up to like over a hundred or a hundred and a quarter dollars or something. Len finally won. And so he opened it and there's the block of ice! I thought Bill was gonna choke Mary! Oh, that block of ice it was so funny! You know you leave it for a few years and everybody forgets and then she does it again! It's for the kids! Over the last couple of years Mary's organized the dinner for the auction (for more than a hundred people). It's a huge feat! When I have to cook for twenty people I'm thinkin' I can't do this! And it's just nothing for her, nothing, nope! Mary's family is very important to her. Especially Niko! They come first!" said Joan.

Homestead Visit

It was late July 2007, within weeks of the death of John Edwards that Mary and Logan set out on the highway for Goodwin, Alberta, leaving the resort in the trusted hands of Connie at the peak of the summer tourist season. Claudia Cherne and Connie had been hammering at Mary to convince her to take two full weeks at the old homestead but she would only commit to a week because she just hates being away from Nimpo for any length of time. Connie hoped Mary would change her mind and relax a bit so she secretly negotiated with her boss to take an extra week off work, just in case.

When they arrived at the old homestead Mary found everything exactly the same as she remembered it. The folks who now owned the land were not around to talk to so she toured the old buildings and went around the old neighborhood looking for familiar faces from a lifetime ago. She knocked on doors and poked her head in as if she'd never been gone. Most people weren't home or had moved away but she did find her old school chum, Norma was home. They visited and chatted about old times for a bit and took photos of the homestead.

Mary held herself together pretty well, at least until she stood at the old house her dad built and remembered how he put those shingles on the roof by hand, one by one. There they all were perfectly in order exactly where he'd nailed them. His hands had roamed all over that roof and he had cut every shingle himself. Even the exterior paint was the same white paint, although it was severely faded and peeling. But those buildings including the old outhouse stood the test of a half-century. And there they all were in front of her, in all their glorious simplicity standing exactly as they did after they were constructed when she was a young girl. It was as if her home had been waiting for her to come back all these years. It was as if her dad was right there working on the roof and she could almost hear his voice. She could sense his presence all over that place. She sensed her mother's voice as she once stood in the doorway wiping her hands on her apron calling her and her sister Hilda into the house for dinner. She ran her hands over the peeling paint and the grain of the exposed wood, then broke down and cried.

She walked out to the fields with the sun on her face to where her father once grew Alfalfa, Wheat, and Barley grasses. She stood wearing her bright red T-shirt, just gazing across the endless sea of vibrant color. The green Wheat grass and the stunning yellow Canola blossoms dancing in the warm breeze that spread as far as the eye could see, were all growing in front of her as if nothing had changed.

Just twenty miles to the east, across the Smokey River was Bezanson, Alberta, where her mother's parents settled their land. Yes, it was all there, the farm, the old buildings, the outhouse, the endless fields and the vast expanse of blue sky, that same horizon she had pondered as a child. Nothing had really changed, except her father and mother were gone. But their essence permeated from the land they had worked, and the life they built for her and Hilda was embedded in the buildings. It was like walking into an old painting on the wall, a time warp of her existence.

The passing-away of so many friends, especially in the last year, and the reality of times gone by probably had a hand in motivating her to not delay in finally making this trip home, possibly for the last time. Physically connecting with her roots, to the past and to her parents had been long overdue, and after this she could set her bearings on the future. Touching base again grounded her for the next phase of her life! She had done what she came to do and now it was time to go home and she could do it with peace in her heart.

No moss grew on the tires as Mary and Logan began their journey back to BC. They were supposed to take a week off but they left on a Thursday and were back home on Saturday night. They were spotted sitting around an open fire in front of the house cooking entimadas with Connie, Niko, Claudia and Frank. Entimadas are basically grilled sandwiches roasted between two hot irons over a campfire.

When asked how their trip went and why they were back so soon, the first words out of Mary's mouth were, "There's no place like home!" And she said it just like Dorothy from the Wizard of Oz too! She was talking about the Chilcotin, not Grande Prairie. This wilderness plateau was where she had raised her own children, worked her own land, built her own adult life. It's the place she formed countless lifelong relationships and bonds. Nimpo Lake was now inextricably as much a part of the fiber of her being as was her childhood homestead. They both looked quite well rested and that seemed a tad-bit odd in light of the fact that they had just driven...no... raced two thousand miles without a break. They arrived sporting a speeding ticket, which was further proof that the visit to the old farm had been swift and deliberate. Ah, but it was well worth it. They had set out not knowing what they'd find, whether Mary's old home would even be there at all. Time and fate had been kind to the old place. It hadn't been torn down, burned down, repainted, or renovated. The hands of the powers-that-be had left it completely alone so Mary could find it once again.

Last Minute Giggles

During the week before submitting Mary's story to my publisher, in the late spring of 2009, she had a special afternoon Happy Hour to celebrate her fortieth year on the plateau and she served a spread of delicious food nibblers and a few spirits. Folks showed up at four o'clock and sat around chatting. One conversation led to another and it came up that Mary had invited someone in for a visit a few days earlier. She'd been working so hard that day and was running on fumes so when she went to serve up some sausage snacks she'd cut up, she accidentally grabbed a handful of something else and plopped it on the plate. She set the plate out on the coffee table and when her guest reached for a piece of sausage he noticed something peculiar and quickly yanked his hand back. "Ah Mary, the sausage is wigglin'," he said. Well Mary took one look at the plate and saw what she'd done. She'd grabbed a handful of fishing worms instead of sausage and served it up for chewin' and those worms were ripe, just squirming away there. It's a good thing the guy had a sense of humor and he and Mary had a roaring laugh over the whole thing. One can only imagine what one's own experience might be. Mary gave herself a pat on the back for that one. After hearing that story and havin' a good chuckle myself, I turned to the local RCMP Sergeant Ken Brissard who was sitting on the next couch munching on some snacks and sipping some Scotch. "Hey, over the winter I saw an RCMP truck out on the lake-ice and I remember thinkin' at the time, who is that crazy guy, was that you out there?" I asked. Of course, being that there are only a small handful of officers in the Nimpo-Anahim area the chances of it having been him were high. "Yeah that probably was me! I think I had a Constable with me at the time. I'll tell ya that was the quietest ride I ever took out there. He was scared we were going to break through the ice, never said a word the whole drive. When I stopped the truck he didn't move an inch. There was no way he was going to step out of the truck. That was Constable AK Puri from Montreal. I told him, there's three feet of ice out there, nothing to worry about! But no, he wasn't going to step out for anything," said Ken.

On a another note, but still a humorous one, Mary's friend Bill Bremmeyer was over visiting and a Hawk swooped down near the house and grabbed her cat Puff-Puff and lifted him eight feet into the air and was fixin' to make a meal of him. But he lost his grip and dropped Puff-Puff and flew up into a tree to reassess his strategy. Well that darn Cat was so mad he climbed up the tree after the Hawk but by the time he managed to climb to just below the spot where the Hawk was sitting, he flew into the next tree. So the Cat climbed down and up the other tree, determined to get him, but the Hawk just flew away.

In the spring of 2009 Mary had to butcher one of her Geese which left the other one wandering around by alone. A young Bald Eagle decided he was gonna make a try for the Goose and poised himself in a low tree branch and prepared to attack. Once the Goose realized what was happening he started barking like a Dog, which confused the Eagle to the point where he backed off. The Goose realized that he needed protection, so he started hanging around with the two Llamas and went everywhere sandwiched between them. It was obvious what he was doin'.

Conclusion

When you meet Mary for the first time a chord is struck. You come away feeling as though you've just been touched by some sort of divine purity you just don't see in the world these days, or with a sense that you've learned something that can help you in some way. You don't always know what it is right away but often later, sometime down the road you might be doing something and she'll flash across your mind. Something she might have said or did touched you viscerally. Her philosophy on life and her sturdy see-anything-through energy can leave you speechless. For her, there is no such word as 'can't'. Many people refer to that ideal in conversation as if they know what it means but to actually put that ethic into practice as a part of a daily routine, to make it part of what you are, is a rare thing. She's a tough act to follow and even if someone wanted to mirror themselves after her it's unlikely they could do it day after day, year after year, decade after decade. It is as if some Angel sent her to the woods to bloom, not to exist in isolation but quite possibly to teach. If she lived in a desert she would be its oasis. Here in the Chilcotin wilderness she is an unwilting Rose that comes to you in the form of a gentle hand. She is a friend to anyone of any breed and political candidates from all persuasions are welcome in her home. After the tragedy of 911 she proudly hoisted the American Flag up beside her Canadian Flag and they have flapped side by side in the wind ever since. She says there should be no borders between people and that unification of countries can't come soon enough for her. She will always be ready with a smile and a bit of food for any strangers that might knock on her door no matter who they are. And no matter what life brings, she quietly makes her rounds cabin to cabin, tent to tent, community to community, bringing gifts of food and a smile to people who would otherwise have no one to talk to because she realizes that even the smallest gesture can make a difference in someone's life!

* * * * *

Mary says that there's a quote by Oprah Winfrey that perfectly reflects how she lives her life.

"Life isn't about what you have; it's about what you have to give!"

Mary Kirner is the Oprah of the wilderness.

* * * * *

The End

Mary burning debris in winter.

Mary and her horse.

Mary picking mushrooms.

Mary cooking for the 139 Club

Mary sitting among wild alpine flowers.

Mary's clan.

Mary and her grandson Niko.

Mary smoking rainbow trout.

Mary hauling lumber for her remote cabin
at Kirner Lake

Mary with Logan and his bare Supercub frame.

Mary and Constable Derek Strong.

Mary baling hay for the Llamas.

Mary's house in summer.

Mary hauling wood in her snow machine.

Mary's pet deer.

Frank and Claudia Cherne and their plane
at Mary's dock.

Mary, Corky Klein, and Mike Kadar getting ready
for a turkey shoot.

Mary's dad's 500 year old house.

Lyman Thompson at the barbeque pit.

Mike Kadar practicing his arm-wrestling techniques.

John Edwards.

Mary's mother sitting on a moose she shot.

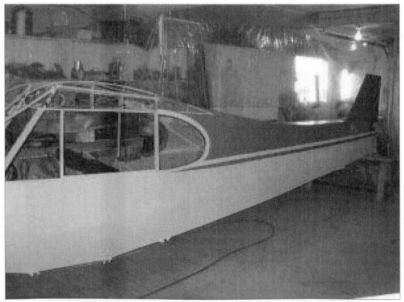

Logan's Supercub refabric project in progress.

Mary's Old Homestead

Mary and her sister Hilda.

Llamas in winter.

Two Fox Kits outside the shop.

The Fisher looking for a meal.

Great Horned Owl in the chicken pen.

Mary bucking a log.

Mary's friend Stan Barrett.

Map of Bob and Jeni Kovacs Icefield route.

Acknowledgments

Thanks to Frank and Claudia Cherne for your authentic smiles and significant story contributions and for tolerating my frequent breakfast interruptions.

Frank and Betty Ayres for allowing me a visit in your home at Anahim, and for the ride to Nimpo when I was truckless after my rollover.

Bill Graham, and son Dwayne from Montana for leaving your snowy tent in September, to come and sit with me in my cabin, for bringing a pot of hot coffee and a fishing rod, and for a wonderful chat about your 39 year fondness for Mary.

Val King, and Joan Smiley for sharing your feelings and experiences with me about Mary.

Lars and Diane from Vancouver, for letting me follow you around during two of your vacations at Mary's with pen, paper, and a tape recorder.

Mary's daughter Connie for allowing me an interview.

Mary's sister Hilda for taking time away from your Trout fishing to provide me with lighthearted conversation about yours and Mary's early years.

Thank you Mary for allowing me into your world and having faith in me, and for the dinners, rides to town for supplies, advice, education, and Happy Hour sipping.

Mary's partner Logan for an interview, photos, as well as many tire changes and computer help.

Thank you to my family for tolerating my extended disappearance: My daughter Jennifer, my son Brandon, my little grandson Aidan, my nephews Troy and Christopher, my mother Virginia, my sisters Naomi and Yvonne, and my grandparents Henry and Alvina, my good friend Janna, and last but definitely not least my hat is off to my constant canine companion-- little fourteen year old Pawkett-Girl who slept vigil under my desk throughout the writing of my manuscript and beyond.